WE ARE THE WORLD
*Globalization and the
Changing Face of Missions*

WE ARE THE WORLD
Globalization and the Changing Face of Missions

J. David Lundy

OM
publishing

Copyright © 1999 J. David Lundy

First published in 1999 by O.M. Publishing

05 04 03 02 01 00 99   7 6 5 4 3 2 1

O.M. Publishing is an imprint of Paternoster Publishing,
PO Box 300, Carlisle, Cumbrian, CA3 0QS, UK
Website–www.paternoster-publishing.com

British Library Cataloguing in Publication Data
A catalogue record for this book is available from the British Library

ISBN 1-85078-342-X

Cover Design by Mainstream, Lancaster
Typeset by WestKey Ltd, Falmouth, Cornwall
Printed in Great Britain by
Caledonian International Book Manufacturing Ltd, Glasgow

Chapters

About the Author

John David Lundy was born in 1949 in the same town as famous missionary Jonathan Goforth: Ingersoll, Ontario in Canada. He grew up in a Christian home in London, Ontario as the oldest of eight children. He committed his life fully to Christ while at university and in 1972 graduated from the University of Toronto with an Honours BA in political science. His first exposure to missions was a summer programme with Operation Mobilisation (OM) in France in 1971. From 1972 until 1978 David served with OM in India as a missionary. During this time he married Linda, a nurse from Toronto. Their only child, Mark, was born in Bombay in 1977.

From 1979 to 1985 David served as the first Canadian Director of Arab World Ministries. His missions' executive leadership role continued when from 1985 to 1994 he served as the Canadian Director for OM.

He continued his academic studies, completing his Master of Divinity degree from Ontario Theological Seminary in 1988. He obtained his Doctor of Ministry degree from Gordon-Conwell Theological Seminary in 1995.

In 1995, David returned to his first love – India. He was drawn by the opportunity to be the architect of and teach in an innovative postgraduate level, cross-cultural school in Hyderabad jointly sponsored by OM-India and Briercrest Biblical Seminary in Canada. He is involved directly in missions this way on a part-time basis, making two visits to India each year. He also pastors a growing church of 150 people in Welland, Ontario as well as conducting training seminars in churches to equip evangelicals in how to share their faith cross-culturally with the increasing number of South Asians now resident in the West who are Hindus, Muslims, and Sikhs.

Foreword

As you will see in the final chapter of this book, David Lundy gives me the last word! It may be a little too kind of the publishers to also allow me an introductory word!!

The most significant change I have witnessed in 25 years of leadership within Operation Mobilisation has been the growth of the Church in the Two-Thirds World and the rise of the Two-Thirds World missionary force. It depends on our exact definition of a missionary but the statisticians assure us that the missionaries from the Two-Thirds World now outnumber those from the First World

This is an almost incredible change because it has taken place so rapidly and it should cause the worldwide Church to rejoice at the greatness of our God and His salvation.

Have missions established in the West and led by Westerners changed in step with what God has been doing in His world? Surely not and this should be a reason for repentance and action.

For many of us, further understanding of the issue is crucial and David's book will surely be an important contribution to an inadequate amount of writing on the issue.

It is particularly important as it presents a significant case study of a mission which in spite of its failings, has sought to globalise. It is obviously vital for us as a mission to reflect upon this material but I also believe there will be real value here for other mission leaders and missiologists.

Like myself, you will probably not agree with all that David writes. I have found myself for examsple yelling 'surely not' when David says, 'Americans should forget Libya' but I'm grateful that essential issues are raised here which require further discussion and action in the mission community.

Peter Maiden,
Associate International Director,
Operation Mobilisation

Introduction

In 1985, Live Aid, a British non-profit making organisation, gathered together popular musicians from all over the world to sing live and to record the song, 'We Are The World'. This song raised money for Ethiopian famine relief. Part of the impact of this much-celebrated event was due to the fact that over one billion people in almost every country of the world watched or listened to the performance simultaneously. 'We Are The World' was an apt title, for the musicians represented a cross-section of the United Nations. Through state-of-the-art technology the communication also had a global and instantaneous impact. 'We Are The World' became an icon of globalization. The experience was global in makeup, global in impact.

Globalization: its meaning came to me in a more crystallised way as a result of a conversation I had a few years ago. 'The growth of Operation Mobilisation can be compared to the maturing of the banyan tree in our beloved country of India,' the Indian man persuasively gesticulated as he endeavoured to describe the nature of globalization of missions to me. 'The branches of the banyan tree drop shoots to the ground which, when taking root, support the parent branches and in turn become trunks, so that one tree covers a very large extent of ground,' he went on to say. Sitting there in Hyderabad, listening to Divakaran philosophise, I couldn't help thinking how this middle-aged national missionary, himself for many years one of the leaders of Operation Mobilisation's massive ministry in India, was the embodiment of globalization of missions.

Three decades previously, in May, 1966, this high-caste Hindu had been aimlessly wandering the streets of New Delhi. Life seemed to hold no purpose for Divakaran, and in his troubled state of mind, he was contemplating suicide. Five months earlier he had gone on a Hindu pilgrimage in his search for inner peace. Nothing happened. He tried to fill the void in his life with many things, like going to the movies. Nothing worked. Life held no meaning for him. His desperation and restlessness became so intense that he could hardly sleep. Although he had passed his entrance exams for university, and had always hoped to study medicine, his deepest longing was to find the answer to the emptiness and lack of peace and joy in his life.

While in New Delhi, he saw a crowd gathered on the street side and he heard noise coming from that general direction, so out of curiosity he wandered over. As he stood at the edge of the crowd, he realised he could understand the language of the person speaking: English. Coming from the southernmost state in India, Kerala, he didn't always understand what was being said here in the Hindi-speaking north. Two young men were speaking in a loud voice about Jesus. After the talk, they gave out some papers and sold some books to the crowd. Out of idle curiosity, Divakaran picked up one of the papers, lying discarded on the ground. It was called 'Life After Death'. Realising his limited rupees weren't going to be of any use to him after he died, he decided to buy one of the Bibles they were selling. On impulse, he quickly wrote down their address and walked off to read the material he had received from these earnest young men.

As it grew dark, Divakaran got onto a bus that took him to the outskirts of the city. Still under a black cloud of despair, he found a lonely wooded spot and quietly drank the two bottles of poison that he had brought along in his pocket. At the same time, he almost unthinkingly gasped out, 'Jesus, if you are the real god, save me from this.' Slipping into a deep stupor, he muttered, 'There is no god.'

Three days later he woke up to find himself in a hospital ward. The fellow who had given him his address on the street corner was standing by Divakaran's bedside. He soon left, putting a copy of Billy Graham's *Peace With God* by Divakaran's bedside. Providentially, Divakaran had been found and given emergency hospital treatment. The police had identified him through his name written inside his new Bible. They then tracked down his two new friends whose address was on a scrap of paper in the Bible – his only other means of identification.

'Through the testimony of these friends, and other believers in Christ, I heard about God's plan of salvation', Divakaran now exclaims. 'Alone on my knees on the evening of May 14, 1966, I put my complete faith in the Lord Jesus Christ. Tears of joy filled my eyes, and I discovered in my heart a deep and true peace that "passes all understanding". Words cannot describe that discovery. It was unspeakable, so full of joy . . . too beautiful to express!'

Those young men who were sovereignly brought into the life of this sincere but troubled Hindu happened to work with Operation Mobilisation (OM). Since Divakaran did not really know any other Christians, the OM workers he had stumbled across discipled him. He soon joined one of OM's evangelism teams. He travelled and ministered with the team along the Ganges River, learning to share his faith with others, to read God's Word reflectively, pray, and live in community with other believers. After several years of discipleship training and service with various OM teams, Divakaran went to seminary for four years where he was theologically grounded and able to develop more ministry skills.

Upon returning to OM after graduation, Divakaran was given leadership responsibilities. Over the intervening years, he held key ministry positions in OM-India, such as: roving Bible teacher, administrative leader for teams in West Bengal and Orissa states, Chief Administrative Officer, and Associate Executive Director. He is now in ministry outside OM.

From OM-India's humble beginnings in 1963, when a truckful of bedraggled Westerners arrived overland from Belgium, not knowing the local language or culture, and not being connected to the Indian church in any way, only sure of their radical brand of discipleship and the message that, 'Jesus

Saves', this ministry has flourished to the point that there are now seven hundred national missionaries in the organisation. It is widely recognised by the Indian church that OM is a credible, evangelical parachurch ministry. Divakaran is an example of a Two-Thirds World national who has held his own in discussions and decision-making circles in OM internationally.[1] Others like him are among the thirty or so nationals in OM-India leadership who are much sought after by other Indian parachurch ministries and churches, let alone by the wider OM family internationally.

Indeed missions have come full circle. Nations which have historically been considered simply the depository of missionaries are now sending their own. Brazil, Nigeria, and Korea (to choose one nation from each of the three major continents evangelised only within the last two hundred years) now send out over ten thousand missionaries each. India, the recipient of the father of the modern missionary movement, William Carey, although still desperately in need of being evangelised, probably has around fifteen thousand missionaries of its own,

---

[1] The term *Two-Thirds World* is to be preferred to other designations, such as the more commonly known *Third World* or *Developing World*. Larry Pate, for example, in his ground-breaking book, *From Every People* (Monrovia, CA: MARC, 1989), pp. 12–13, sees this as the most suitable term to use because it doesn't imply cultural, economic, or developmental superiority of the Western World. The term *Two-Third World* delineates the approximately two-thirds of the world's population and land mass found in the continents of Latin America, Asia, Africa, as well as Oceania. *Two-Thirds World* sounds less pejorative than the other terms, while enabling a useful distinction to be made in relation to the peoples of Europe and North America, who have substantially different histories and cultures than the other blocs of the world's population which, although dissimilar from each other in significant ways, nevertheless, have substantive affinities with each other. Using *Two-Thirds World* is not without problems, however, in that, as Patrick Johnstone points out in *Operation World* (5th edition, Grand Rapids, MI: Zondervan, 1993), p. 21, about 86 per cent of the world's population was to be found in the Two-Thirds World by 1995 (not 66 per cent!). Similar problems of accurate designation exist for the sometimes favoured terms *North* (Western World) and *South* (Two-Thirds World). All things considered, what is readily observable is that, as Peter Wagner maintains (in M. L. Nelson, ed., *Readings in Third World Missions: A Collection of Essential Documents* (Pasadena, CA: William Carey Library, 1978), p. 62, the non-Western World seems to form a psychological block due to a common desire for independence from the Western World. Although not an ideal term, *Two-Thirds World* is the one we will use in this book.

depending on whom you talk to.[2] The church in the Two-Thirds World is an increasingly major player in the sphere of world missions. With ever-growing frequency, churches in the West are being challenged to stop sending missionaries and start sending money. After all, we are told, we can get a national to do the job for one-tenth of the cost of sending one of our own!

Is this a passing fad or is the rise of the Two-Thirds World missionary force here to stay? It is the contention of this book that not only is this a trend which is here to stay, but that it is one of the most significant developments in world missions in the last two hundred years. That being the case: the job of evangelising the lost must be globalised. Just what globalisation is, in relation to the world of missions, will be the subject of careful scrutiny in this book.

---

[2] We will define what we mean by the term *missionary* in chapter two. Indian Missions Association claims that at the end of 1996 there were fifteen thousands nationals in India who were missionaries (*Indian Missions*. Oct.–Dec., 1996), p. 24.

ONE

The Fourth and Final Era of Missions?

Apurva Tiwari was born on October 14, 1973 in North India.[1] He has two younger brothers, and one older sister. His father is a farmer and village pradhan (elder). The family is staunchly Hindu. Shiva is a Hindu deity devotedly followed in the area. Apurva received a Gospel portion in 1988 through an Indian Evangelical Mission missionary. After reading this tract, he came to know the Lord. In 1990, Apurva joined an OM team and worked in another part of North India. When he next visited home he was badly beaten up and admitted to hospital for a few days, all because of declaring himself for Christ.

Now having completed the basic OM training programme in evangelism, Apurva and a friend, Vipul, work among high-caste Hindus in Orissa in church planting. Orissa is one of the most Hindu of all Indian states. The Hindu deity Shiva is ardently worshipped and pilgrims come from all over India to its famous shrines and temples.

Apurva is a new breed of missionary. Dressed in the traditional garb of Brahmins and refusing to eat meat, Apurva and Vipul meet people in the shops, and in their homes. They are not white-skinned foreigners, but nationals, those who know the language, don't struggle with the local food, are used to living simply, and fit in to the culture. They are unobtrusively getting the job done.

---

[1] The following story is taken from *OM India News*, [summer1996], p. 4.

Arpurva delights in telling the story of one of the people he meets in the course of his every day visitation. 'One day a weaver came to join our discussion. I began telling him some of the miracles, how Jesus took the five chapatis (loaves of bread) and two fish, and fed five thousand people. The weaver asked how the universe was made and I shared the story of creation.

During the next three months this man often came to our weekly meetings and he accepted Christ as his Lord and Saviour. He started telling people about Jesus, and praying for the sick, some of whom were healed. Now he goes from village to village preaching. He and his wife were recently baptised. They have four children and are bringing them up knowing the Word of God,' he matter-of-factly tells the story. Many have been won to the Lord by their own people, as was Apurva, himself a product of national missionary work. But let's consider how we got to this marvellous place in the history of missions.

Missiologists tend to ascribe the beginning of modern, Protestant missions as we know it today to William Carey's publishing of his treatise: *An Enquiry Into the Obligations of Christians To Use Means For the Conversion of the Heathen* and his sailing to India in 1792. Carey's writings and example pricked the conscience of the British church and resulted in a number of parachurch and denominational mission societies being formed to launch thousands of missionaries to take the Gospel to the distant shores of Latin America, Africa, and Asia, seemingly for the first time. In analysing subsequent mission history, some missiologists, such as Ralph Winter, have identified two other eras, or turning points.[2] The next came two generations later when Hudson Taylor captured the imagination of the church in Europe and North America, this time with a vision for evangelising the interiors of the vast countries where until then only the coastal cities had been reached. Thus began a proliferation of new mission societies such as Sudan Interior Mission, Regions Beyond Missionary Union, and Africa Inland Mission which, as their names infer, signified their modus operandi.

---

[2] Ralph Winter, 'The Long Look: Eras of Mission History.' In *Perspectives on the World Christian Movement*, Steven Hawthorne and Ralph Winter eds (Pasadena, CA: William Carey Library, 1983), pp. 167–177.

Finally, in the 1930s, through the insights of missionary statesmen like William Cameron Townsend and Donald McGavaran, an idea took shape that saw evangelising of the unreached not just in terms of the two hundred or so *nations* of the world, but of the people groups within those nations. A multitude of unreached people groups may exist within one country, so the reasoning went, that is, among those bound by an identical linguistic, cultural bond which may be entirely different from their neighbour's. The pioneering work of men like McGavaran and Townsend spawned a new generation of missions, such as Wycliffe Bible Translators, Gospel Recordings, and New Tribes Mission. Their new way of configuring the task of world evangelisation was refined by institutions such as the US Centre For World Missions. This resulted in a refocused effort to reach the lost, and added fresh momentum to the missionary cause. It also forced the church to face the fact that the fulfillment of the Great Commission had a long way to go: establishing a viable church in each of the thousands of people groups was far more complicated and detailed than when *ethne* (Mt. 28:19; Rom. 16:26) was understood to refer only to *nations*.

What better timing then than today to discover that it will take the whole church to reach the whole world for Christ?! When a respected missions' spokesman, Ted Yamamori, claims that we need a minimum of one hundred thousand new tentmakers to bring closure to world evangelisation, it's time for the church in the Western World to admit that it doesn't have the momentum and vitality to get the job done alone.[3] Besides, who said it was our job anyway? Wasn't the commitment to make disciples of all nations given to all who would claim to be Christ's disciples, regardless of skin colour, or ability to speak English?!

By the 1980s the Two-Thirds World church bypassed the Western World church in sheer numbers for the first time since the days of the early church. By 1990, 62 per cent of the global church was found in the parts of the world that had hitherto been considered unevangelised and worthy only of receiving

---

[3] Ted Yamamori, *God's New Envoys* (Portland, OR: Multnomah Books, 1987), p. 58.

missionaries, as compared to making up only 42 per cent of the worldwide church in 1960.[4] It is estimated that by the century's end, this lopsided population in favour of the Two-Thirds World church will have increased to 77 per cent.[5]

Together with this rapid growth of the Two-Thirds World church, has been the increase in the number of missionaries being sent out by the Two-Thirds World church. Keyes and Pate have traced this phenomenal growth from missionaries in 1960 to an anticipated 164,000 by AD 2000.[6] This is what Walter Buhlmann, in 1977, had labelled as the *Third* church seizing the day. He had called the Two-Thirds World church *Third*, not in the sense of significance, but chronologically, in that it was the end product of missionary activity which had seen the Gospel transplanted first from Asia to Europe, and then from Europe back to Asia, etc.[7]

A paradigm shift in power from the West to the East can be seen as inevitable as numerically the momentum shifts, whether viewed in terms of overall church population or the sheer size of the missionary force. Speaking of missionaries, Pate's research indicates that the non-Western missionary force is growing at the rate of 13 per cent per year.[8] The number of their missionary agencies also has increased, from 743 in 1980 to 1094 in 1989.[9] By comparison, during the 1980s the Western missionary movement grew at a rate of 4 per cent per annum, whereas the Two-Thirds World movement grew at 12 per cent.[10]

Furthermore, through the pace-setting work in the last several decades of groups such as Partners International (previously Christian Nationals Evangelism Commission), the Anglo-American church has been sensitised to this trend of

---

[4] Johnstone, *Operation World*, p. 25.
[5] *Ibid.*, pp. 25–26.
[6] Larry Keyes and Larry Pate, 'Two-Thirds World Missions: The Next 100 Years,' *Missiology: An International Review* 21(2) (April 1993), pp. 187–206.
[7] Walter Buhlmann, *The Coming of the Third Church*. (Maryknoll, NY: Orbis Books, 1977).
[8] Pate, *Missiology*, p. 16.
[9] *Ibid.*, p. 17.
[10] *Ibid.*, p. 45.

supporting *national* missionaries.[11] More recently, iconoclastic groups like Christian Aid Mission and Gospel For Asia have caught the attention of the Western World church through slogans like, 'Support a native missionary for one-tenth of what it costs to send an American'. The church in the West has been forced not only to face up to the reality of the expensive proposition of sending its own people into missions overseas, but also to the question of whether it ought to be in the business of sending missionaries at all!

Throughout this book I will be giving many illustrations of what I am talking about, mostly through using Operation Mobilisation (OM) as a microcosm of the bigger picture. I have spent the better part of two decades in OM. I have watched it move from its adolescent years when I joined in 1971 to its adulthood today. As OM grew from its modest beginnings in 1957 when three Bible college students went to Mexico to proclaim Christ on their summer vacation, to its present membership of 2800 missionaries drawn from over seventy different countries and working in about an equal number, the complexity of its internationality has also become greater. Among these short-term and career missionaries, over one-third are from the Two-Thirds World. Korea is probably the fastest growing sending arm of OM, with two hundred missionaries on the field.[12]

A glimpse at the pie chart in a recent edition of OM's in-house magazine, *Relay*, reveals that only 52 per cent of OM missionaries come from our traditional recruiting fields of North America and Europe with 48 per cent coming from what is classified as the Two-Thirds World.

---

[11] The term *national* is generally used in missions' circles to refer to people from the Two-Thirds World. We will use it in the same way, although technically speaking we are all nationals of some country or another. The continued use of *native* with reference to missionaries from the Two-Thirds World by missionary statesmen like K. P. Yohannan is to be discouraged because it tends to perpetuate the all-too-common derogatory or condescending attitude initiated by Western colonists. *National* should only be used to refer to missionaries working as evangelists or church planters in their own country. *Evangelists* work in or outside their own culture, whereas *missionaries* only work cross-culturally. In that sense, not all *nationals* working in an unreached area can be classified as *missionaries*.

[12] Unless otherwise noted, all such statistics of OM are taken from its *Personnel 1996* records.

Interestingly enough, India is OM's largest provider of missionaries, with six hundred adults, the United States and Great Britain respectively fielding the next largest numbers. Most of India's OM missionaries do work in their own country, but usually not in their own culture and language, so they do qualify as genuine missionaries. For instance, Marcus Chacko, now a respected Indian missionary, went from his home in Kerala to Rajasthan in 1971, not aware of all the cultural adjustments he would have to make. He had to adjust to eating chapatis instead of rice, speaking Hindi instead of Malayalam (let alone English), and living in extreme heat or cold instead of constant tropical heat.

OM gives every appearance of being a large mission agency with more of an international mix of missionaries in its work force than seen in most comparable organisations, except Youth With a Mission (YWAM).[13] With this in mind, OM serves as a useful model in assessing some of the issues that globalisation of missions will face in the coming years. That is why we refer to it so frequently in this book. What OM faces today other Anglo-American rooted missions will face tomorrow. As we reflect on the changing face of missions – often using OM as a litmus test of trends with respect to globalisation – we will discover some unusual dynamics that historical missions have apparently not really begun to understand, or fully grappled with, in their triumphant march to completing the task of world evangelisation. We will discover, for instance, that *internationalisation* and *globalisation* are not exactly the same thing. A mission can be very international in make-up and yet not be truly globalised. We will be faced with the principle that

---

[13] Appendix 2 of *Operation World* provides a useful breakdown by nationality of the membership of 116 Protestant missions. Peri Rickard of YWAM writes in *Internationalising Missionary Training* (Grand Rapids, MI: Baker Book House, 1991), p. 161, that in 1989 YWAM had 35 per cent of its workers from the Two-Thirds World. This is comparable to OM's 1994 statistic, which suggests that YWAM may currently be even more international in composition than OM. By comparison, an older faith mission, WEC, of its 1602 members in 1992 coming from 43 countries, had only 12.5 per cent coming from the Two-Thirds World and it was thought that this percentage was not likely to increase beyond 20 per cent by the year AD 2000 (statistics taken from a letter written to me by the International Secretary, Dr. Dietrich Kuhl, dated April 12, 1995).

true partnership with the Two-Thirds World church means more than giving money. Commitment of finances to organisations specialising in support of nationals will therefore require more careful scrutiny. We will venture the insight that the internal culture and ethos of mission agencies must change if the Two-Thirds World church and mission leaders are not to bypass existing Western World structures and get the job done on their own, often repeating the mistakes of their predecessors. Oriental participation in a mission does not mean Orientals feel at home when the organisation operates by British time-management principles, is ambivalent to authority figures, is not very relational, and handles the resolution of disputes confrontationally.

You may not be interested in every aspect of the discussion about globalisation of missions. I suspect that the Christian public is especially concerned with how to be a good steward of scarce missions' money. If so, then the chapters that pertain to the consideration of the issue of the support of nationals will be essential reading for you. Skip, if need be, the chapters on internal internationalisation of missions. At the same time, if you work on a church missions' committee, or are a missionary candidate choosing a mission, then those hidden dimensions of missionary organisations are ones you need to know about. But first, let's look at what globalisation means from a biblical standpoint.

TWO

A Biblical Consideration of Globalisation

What does Wimpeys have to do with globalisation? I was amazed recently, on one of my biannual visits to Hyderabad in India to teach in a post-graduate school, to discover that the fast-food giant, Wimpeys, had come to the centre of town. A few years ago it would have been unheard of for such a multinational corporation (let alone one that offered beef products for consumption!) to show its head in what has remained a largely traditional, Hindu country. Ironically, Wimpeys had not come to my town of residence in Canada, Welland, just down the road from Niagara Falls.

Such is the breath-taking speed at which our world has been altered and unified by such marvels as the computer, to name just one cause of globalisation. We should not be surprised to see a Sting T-shirt on a female teenager in Beijing, even if the nation she lives in is somewhat anti-Western. Nor should we be puzzled when a Saudi Arabian intones the Koran in one breathe and in the next turns to his friend to talk about the latest Gucci fashion styles. Globalisation seems to be here to stay!

Globalisation has become a buzz word in contemporary culture. In fact it is used so frequently, and in so many different ways, that it seems to have been emptied of exact meaning. John Naisbitt, popular futurist, wrote a best-seller embodying the notion of globalisation's in its title, *Global Paradox*. The nuances of globalisation are not what they appear to be at first glance. We've come a long way since receiving the revelation from Canadian communications' guru, Marshall McLuhan, that the world lives in a global village. This chapter will examine globalisation within such fields as economics, management theory, missiology, communications, and education. Suffice it to say at this point that the term has a cluster of meanings, which explains its elasticity of usage, and accounts for some of the lack of clarity over its meaning. We'll work backwards in a sense, starting with the definition used in this book and then explaining how we came up with that definition. What do we mean by globalisation? Especially when we use the term 'christianly'?

> Globalisation is the cultivation of a mindset and the practical expression of it, whereby a group or an individual moves away from parochialism to universalism. In missions, this means that true partnership and synergy emerge between the diverse sides of the worldwide church in the task of world evangelisation.

Unity of Humankind

There are several biblical principles that impinge on the concept of globalisation. An important one is the *unity of humankind*. A fundamental assertion concerning the validity of globalisation for the Christian and missions is based on the principle that one of God's intentions for the human race is unity. By unity we mean that racial, sexual, and cultural relationships are marked by equality and harmony. Major distinctions are found in the creation order between humankind and other animal life (Gen. 1:26), but not between human and human (Gen. 11:1). As John Stott says in *Issues Facing Christians Today*: 'The one people were to populate and tame the one earth, in order to harness its resources to their service. There was no hint at the beginning of the partitioning of the earth or of rivalry between nations.'[1] In the same vein, but now relating harmony to the cross instead of creation, Peter Beyerhaus defends the concept of the unity of humankind when he says, 'Because of Christ's Atonement, all

---

[1] John Stott, *Issues Facing Christians Today* (Bombay: Gospel Literature Service, 989), p. 128.

distinctions of sex, wealth, race, nationality, culture, and language no longer have the power of separation.'[2]

The Fall ushers in the divisions between human beings which have become so familiar to us that we have immunised ourselves against their presence and impact (Gen. 3:7; 4:1–8; 11:1–9). The dawning of the Church Age clarifies God's original intention: in the horizontal relationships found in the Body of Christ – the church, 'There is neither Jew nor Greek, slave nor free, male nor female, for you are all one in Christ Jesus' (Gal. 3:28, Jn. 17:20–23).[3] Interestingly enough, this text in Galatians is applied most frequently today, or so it would seem, to issues of gender equality. But we also need to remind ourselves that it addresses the need for racial equality in the church – a matter of great importance when considering globalisation of missions.

We need to realise the theological importance of the concept of unity of the human race: this dynamic in human relationships is a reflection of the very nature of God Himself. Throughout Scripture we are shown the plurality and yet oneness of the Godhead. The unity of this three-in-one God is nowhere more acutely applied to our human relationships than in John 17 – a passage of great significance, given that it is the last recorded prayer of our Lord prior to the crucifixion narratives. In that High-Priestly prayer Jesus exposes the intimacy of the relationship he has with his heavenly Father, referring to it as being so close as to make them 'one' (vv. 12, 21, 22). In each case where the Father-Son relationship is described in this way, there is an immediate correlation made with Christ's followers who need to mirror the same oneness in their relationships with each other as they see existing in the Trinity. The culmination of this relationship is described as 'complete unity'. Such a human expression of unity cannot fail to have an evangelistic impact on the unchurched: 'My prayer for all of them is that they will be of one heart and mind . . . [so] the world will believe you sent me' (v. 21, *Living Bible*) and 'I in them and you in me, all being perfected into one – so that the world will know you sent me and will understand that you love them as much as you love

[2] Peter Beyerhaus, *Shaken Foundations: Theological Foundations For Mission* (Grand Rapids, MI: Zondervan Publishing House, 1972), p. 94.
[3] Unless otherwise noted, all quoted Scripture is from *The New Internationa* *Version*.

me' (v. 23, *Living Bible*). One conclusion that we might draw from this passage, then, is that globalisation of missions is a laudable goal in that it provides a testimony to the unsaved of the power and authenticity of the Gospel (Jn. 13:35). An Algerian Muslim seeing a Zairian Christian working alongside a French missionary, without there being any discrimination or lovelessness between the two, even though Zaire once was a French colony like Algeria, should speak volumes.

Great pains are taken in the book of Acts to make it clear that racial division has no place in the church. Almost two full chapters are given over to demonstrating that God is impartial with respect to race (10:1–11:18). Peter leads the way, as a result of a vision received from heaven, in showing that Gentile believers have as much right to be considered full-fledged members of the church as do Jewish believers in Christ. Furthermore, Gentile believers are not required to adapt to the cultural and religious customs of their Jewish counterparts (Acts 15:6–20).

Along with this teaching in the book of Acts, in Galatians Paul argues for the Gospel to be viewed as supra-cultural. He chides Peter (who should have known better by this time) that Gentile believers must not be forced to be circumcised or eat kosher meat in order to be treated as true believers, otherwise the grace of God and their freedom in Christ will be nullified (Chapter 2; cf. Acts 15:1–30). Similarly, in our concern to esteem the local church, let us not ignore or be ambivalent to the catholicity and universality of the global church. The church of Jesus Christ is found, underground or visibly, in virtually every country worldwide, if not quite yet in every people group. The Gentile-Jewish struggle in the first century AD reminds us that we must not allow cultural particulars to be made into universals; as this would be a sign of legalism, or of failure to contextualise evangelism. Nor must biblical universals be reduced to optional particulars, which breed licence, or syncretism. To put it another way, as we plant churches cross-culturally, in our concern to work indigenously, let us not ignore the fact that the Gospel critiques culture even if it does not produce one *biblical* culture.[4]

---

[4] Charles Kraft and T. N. Wisley, eds. *Readings in Dynamic Indigenity* (Pasadena, ᑕA: William Carey Library, 1979), p. 89.

Unity is expressed in various ways. It would not be the recommendation made here that unity be equated with parity.
However, unity should be expressed, surely, in terms of functional, if not precise, equality. Myung Hyuk Kim in *Partners in
the Gospel* captures this sense of there needing to be a kind of
practical equality in mission partnerships when he persuasively
argues that:

> Partnership does not mean that each party should be
> equal in terms of ability or possession. It means that each
> party is given its own unique status and tasks. One talent
> and five talents are not equal from a human standpoint,
> but they can be regarded equal from God's point of
> view.[5]

Therefore, a British mission organisation wanting to partner
with the Ugandan church in ministering to the country's tens
of thousands ravaged by AIDS must not insist on the same
number of workers or the same amount of money being
provided by both partners, in its effort to establish an 'equal'
partnership – that would be to impose an artificial, statistical
meaning to partnership.

The sense in which God treats all humankind impartially is
apparent when an analysis is made of the New Testament (NT)
word *prosopolaphia* and its cognates, which translate as *favouritism* or *partiality*. Five of its seven occurrences in the NT refer to
God, declaring him to be totally impartial in his dealings with
all people (Rom. 2:11; Eph. 6:9; Col. 3:25; 1 Pet. 1:17; Acts 10:34).
In two places where *prosopolaphia* is used with respect to
people, both in the same passage, the clear teaching is that it is
sinful to show favouritism in one's dealings with people – in
this case in discriminating between rich and poor church members (Jas. 2:1–13). Fascinatingly enough, *prosopolaphia* and its
two related NT words, according to Arndt and Gringrich, are
used only by early Christian writers, perhaps suggesting that

---

[5] 'Principles of Two-Thirds World Mission Partnerships.' in *Partners in the
Gospel*, eds. James Kraakevik and Dotsey Welliver (Wheaton, IL: Billy Graham
Center, 1991), p. 138.

the idea of impartiality in the Graeco-Roman world of Jesus' day was a foreign one.[6]

Three words in the Old Testament (OT) are translated as *partiality* and *show partiality*, depending on whether the verbal or substantive form of the terms is used. The word *masso* is used in II Chronicles 19:7 and points to the singular impartiality of God in matters of justice. The word *nakar* is used always with respect to people; the Israelites are never to show partiality, whether to a foreigner or a downtrodden one of their own people (Deut. 1:17; 16:19; Prov. 24:23; 28:21).

Finally, *nasa* is used with reference to people (Lev. 19:15) and God (2 Sam. 14:14; Lam. 4:16) – in each case revealing that favouritism is to be uncharacteristic of God's people. Differences between human beings do exist, but differentiations are not to be the basis for treating people unevenly, that is, discriminatorily.

An obvious metaphor for conveying the principle of equality of status before God in the church is the *Body of Christ*. In the Body of Christ differences of function but not differences of status are allowed for. In one of the key passages referring to the Body of Christ, I Corinthians 12:12–27, Paul see-saws back and forth between focusing on the unity of the Body and its diversity. One thing is certain. He does not see distinctions in the Body, in the sense of there existing differing spiritual gifts, as providing a rationale for treating members of the Body differently (vv. 15–26). Equality and uniformity are therefore not to be understood as being synonymous. They are mutually inclusive and form the basis of edification and mutual enrichment; not discrimination or competition. Equality is displayed in the Body by esteem for one another (vv. 22, 23), letting each member make his or her contribution through gifting (vv. 24, 25), and caring for one another (v. 26). Notice Paul's use of the word *equality* in the text of II Corinthians 8:13–16 in relation to financial sharing. When we are willing to share our hard-earned money with the

---

[6] William Bauer, *A Greek-English Lexicon of the New Testament and Other Early Christian Literature*, trans. by W. Arndt and F. Gringrich 2nd ed. (Chicago: The University of Chicago Press, 1979), p. 760.

less fortunate of our brothers and sisters in Christ, we treat them
as equals. Such an attitude, as we shall see, has a significant bearing on the whole issue of financial sharing with Two-Thirds
World national missionaries.

Equality of believers is also radically taught in Ephesians 2.
In a sense, Ephesians 2:11–21 can be viewed as the watershed
passage on the subject of the unity of the church in the NT. It is a
clear exposition of how Christ has broken down racial and cultural barriers. These racial and cultural barriers are in evidence
in the Jewish-Greek (Gentile) animosity displayed throughout
Scripture. In today's world such tensions are only too prevalent, whether between Germans and French in continental
Europe, whites and blacks in the United States, Dravidians and
Aryans in India, Scots and English in Great Britain, or
Quebecois and Anglophones in Canada. The message to the
combatants is the same: 'For He himself is our peace, who has
made the two one and has destroyed the barrier, the dividing
wall of hostility' (v. 14).

What makes the Ephesians passage so powerful in reflecting on the issue is that a literal physical barrier separating Jew
from Gentile in worship had existed for centuries in the temple
in Jerusalem. This *barrier* (a word found only here in the NT) or
dividing wall was a stone wall partitioning the temple proper
from the Court of the Gentiles. Above the entrance leading into
the inner temple was an inscription written in Latin and Greek
that forbade any foreigner (read Gentile) from entering, on
pain of death.[7] Perhaps there could have been no more dra-
matic illustration of the efficacy of the death of Christ in reconciling inveterate enemies into a unified 'God's household' (v.
19), therefore, than in showing that Jew and Gentile could be
brought together harmoniously. In this commentary, Foulkes
makes the point that although the Jews did admit Gentiles as
proselytes into the temple, Jews made their entry so difficult
that the Gentiles' sense of alienation and of being outsiders
was never totally eradicated.[8]

---

[7] Francis Foulkes, *The Epistle of Paul to the Ephesians* (Grand Rapids, MI: W.B
Eerdmans Publishing Co., 1993), p. 81.
[8] *Ibid.*, p. 79.

Perhaps we should be asking ourselves if in the church today there are those whom we accept 'on paper' but whom we treat, in subtle ways, as misfits. Perhaps those with not quite as good an education as ours? Those who don't dress in their 'Sunday best'? And what about those 'immigrants'? Let's face it: The Jewish-Gentile problem is still with us. Relating this passage to racial reconciliation to be found in the church, Fong articulates the same basic thought when he says: 'This international blend of two formerly distinct groups that once thrived on mutual animosity toward each other demonstrates the divine intent to formulate a Church comprised of a single people. . . . These two groups . . . now share something in common with each other that surpasses their [cultural, ethnic, and social] differences.'[9]

Furthermore, the matter at hand is extremely relevant to our primary topic, that is, the globalisation of missions. On the one hand, we may welcome Nigerian and Brazilian missionaries to work alongside us (Westerners) in the task of world evangelisation, but who has to conform to whose ways of going about it? Who are assumed to be the experts? There's more than meets the eye here in applying the principle of the unity of the church to the realm of missions!

One of the issues which must be faced by international missions (and the Western World churches who are still their primary sponsors) is that nationals do not always feel at home in agencies which have Western-derived structures and values. Could such agencies be guilty of a subtle form of racism in much the same way as the early church, which was significantly Jewish and had to grapple with the temptation to retain old prejudices in accepting the 'new kids on the block' – the Gentile believers? Such *hostility* in all its forms must be *put to death* (v. 16). Hostility must give way to fellowship; alienation to harmony; prejudice to respect.

---

[9] Bruce Fong, 'Addressing the Issue of Racial Reconciliation According to the Principles of Eph 2:11–22,' *Journal of the Evangelical Theological Society* 38(4) December, 1995): 565–566.

Partnership in Ministry

A spin-off effect of unity in the church (or in a mission agency) is mutuality in ministry. Such mutuality can also be denoted as *partnership*. Especially as we consider intercultural relationships in missions, a biblical theology of partnership needs to be enunciated. The notion of partnership is so crucial to the globalisation of missions that it will be dealt with here as a separate principle rather than be subsumed under unity. This concept of partnership, when reflecting on globalisation of missions, is the one most frequently referred to in missions' literature.

A word study of *koinonia* is relevant to a biblical understanding of the concept of partnership. Its noun form appears 17 times in the NT and is translated as *fellowship* (the most frequent translation), *sharing, administration, generosity*, and *partnership*. A verbal participle form, found twice, adds, in the one case, the sense of *to be participants* (I Cor. 10:20). Eight times the verbal form, *koinoneo*, is found, and in all but one case, is translated as *share*. Do you get the sense of togetherness, of partnership, that the term seeks to engender?

Another set of words which are translated the same way as *koinoneo* comes from the root word *echo*, literally meaning *to have*. They are *metecho*, translated as *share* or *participate in; metocha*, translated *as sharing* or *participation*; and *metochos*, variously translated as *partaking, sharing, participating, a partner*, or *companion*.[10] Again the sense of close interpersonal identification comes through in the use of the word.

Whichever of these root words is used in Scripture, it is evident that a partnership is involved, whether between God and humans (1 Cor. 1: 9), between individuals (1 Jn. 1: 7), or between churches (2 Cor. 8:4). Qualities of these partnerships include intimacy (1 Jn. 1:3), identification with the other (1 Cor. 10:16), sharing (Phil. 1:5), and fellowship (Gal. 2:9). Schattenmann claims that *koinonia* is a term used in the Hellenistic world to mean unbroken fellowship between the gods and men or

---

[10] 'Koinonia' in *Dictionary of New Testament Theology*, Vol. 1, ed. Colin Brow (Grand Rapids, MI: Zondervan Publishing Co., 1986), pp. 639–640.

between men (as in Plato's *Republic* in his sketching of the ideal community), but is not used in the Septuagint (Greek transla-tion of the OT) to denote the relationship between God and humankind.[11] He also makes the noteworthy observation that Paul never uses the word *koinonia* in a secular sense but always spiritually.

Little wonder then that Two-Thirds World mission leaders emphasise the importance of global partnership being fleshed out not just in terms of strategic and financial arrangements, which is often the Western preoccupation, but through rich, interpersonal relationships. Samuel Escobar, noted Latin mis-siologist and theologian, in particular makes a telling statement when he says: 'Relationship precedes function, friendship precedes efficiency. . . . Trust and friendship presuppose acceptance of the other as an equal partner, acceptance of the humanity and the basic dignity of the other.'[12] He has grasped the thrust of the term *partnership*. Interdependence is not some-thing that suggests weakness in relationships, but a mutuality where each member in the partnership is cherished and released for ministry (1 Cor. 12:21–27).

It must be remarked that, on the other hand, *partnership* can also be used in a pragmatic sense. Seven times Paul uses *koinonia* or its cognates to refer to financial partnership (1 Cor. 8:4; Phil. 1: 5 (translated as *partnership*); 2 Cor. 9:13; Rom. 15:27; Gal. 6:6; Phil. 4:15; 1 Tim. 6:18). Financial sharing, then, is not an insignificant application of genuine partnership. This issue will be taken up again shortly, but for now let us ask whether the 'Three-Self Movement' – a popular missionary strategy of recent generations (which has never been fully repudiated), with its stress on financial independence of emerging Two-Thirds World churches, is a biblical concept, or whether it is based on Anglo-American notions of individualism and power?

Whatever we may conclude, this sense in partnership of mutuality or sharing, carries with it the biblical idea of

---

[11] *Ibid.*, p. 643.
[12] Samuel Escobar, 'The Internationalization of Missions and Leadership Style' (speech to the 1991 Evangelical Foreign Mission Association Annual Convention).

reciprocity in relationships. This notion of *reciprocity* is clearly conveyed in Scripture when it describes the way Christian marriages are supposed to function. Ephesians 5:22–33 reveals that there are privileges and responsibilities on both sides of the marital relationship – which is at the heart of what is meant by reciprocity. Responsibilities include honour and submission on the part of the wife (vv. 22–24, 33), and headship and love on the part of the husband (vv. 25–29, 33). Mutual privileges include sexual intimacy (v. 31), love (v. 25), and respect (v. 33).

Likewise, in global-mission partnerships, as Paul McKaughan explains, such dynamics should be found when reciprocity is at work:

> Partnerships should always be based on perceived mutual benefits to both parties. Many times the benefits may not be the same for all the participants in the partnership. . . . All need a realistic appraisal of their assets, their liabilities, and their needs. This appraisal needs to be done from my perspective, and then I need to look at the issue from the perspective of my future partner.[13]

If global partnerships are to take on the biblical nuances of reciprocity, then structures must be flexible and decisions made through consensus because partnerships are built on human relationships.

What are some of the other biblical aspects of the term partnership? First of all, a commitment to truthfulness in relationships (Mt. 5:37). Cultural differences aside, truthfulness is a godly characteristic in any Christian. We should therefore expect that field reports from nationals back to supporting churches are accurate, and conversely, that donor partner expectations are clear from the outset of a co-operative venture. Such an emphasis will probably require a great deal of communication back and forth. Luis Bush, former International Director of Partners International and now head of the AD 2000 Movement, stresses this feature of global partnerships when he

---

[13] 'A North American Response to Patrick Sookhdeo.' in *Kingdom Partnership for Synergy in Missions*, ed. William Taylor (Pasadena, CA: William Carey Library, 1994), p. 76.

says, 'It is essential that partners communicate frequently, freely and personally in order to avoid misunderstanding.'[14] Honesty in relationships will obviate tensions in the cross-cultural give and take, and pave the way for genuine friendship. Certainly it has been my experience that friendship bonds with Indians I have been in leadership relationships with in India deepened when a breakthrough came as a result of frank and open sharing with one another. Depending on how the quest for honesty is approached, this dynamic of bonding following the trust engendered by openness reaches across cultures.

Related to truthfulness is vision. In referring to the Philippian believers as being in partnership with him (Phil. 1:5), Paul states the importance of them having the same goal and mind as himself (2:1–2; 3:12–17). Sharing a common vision makes for strong partnerships.[15]

Also related to truthfulness is accountability. Throughout Scripture, it is evident that, vertically, humankind is accountable to God, beginning with the Garden of Eden episode in Genesis and ending with the Judgement Seat of Christ scenario in Revelation. Horizontally, it is fleshed out in such settings as the church (Mt. 18:15–17), governments (Rom. 13:1–7), and the family (Col. 3:18–21). Hence, we should not dismiss a pressuring toward mutual accountability in intercultural partnerships as evidence per se of a colonial or imperialistic mentality being foisted on Two-Thirds World participants.

Araujo defines accountability as 'a willingness to place oneself under someone else's review and examination concerning one's motives, actions, and outcomes according to mutually agreed upon expectations, in an atmosphere of good faith and mutual trust.'[16] Accountability breeds trust, which in turn feeds the cultivation of friendship. We see accountability demonstrated in Paul's administration of the 'Jerusalem Relief Fund'

---

[14] Luis Bush and Lorry Lutz, *Partnering in Ministry: The Direction of World Evangelism* (Downer's Grove, IL: Inter Varsity Press, 1990), p. 52.

[15] Bush has an excellent chapter in the above book, *Partnering*, in relating the message of Philippians to partnership. He also makes the point about the importance of common vision in Kraakevik and Welliver, *Partners*, p. 7.

[16] In Taylor, *Kingdom*, 1994, p. 121.

when he declares: 'We want to avoid any criticism of the way we administer this liberal gift. For we are taking pains to do what is right, not only in the eyes of the Lord but also in the eyes of men' (2 Cor. 8:20–21). One of the strengths of OM's partnership between Two-Thirds and Western World sides is that it has a built-in accountability structure. More detail about how that works will be included in a later chapter. Sadly, such fiscal accountability is somewhat lacking in some of the organisations specialising in support of nationals. In these latter cases, proper accountability is inadequately provided by sporadic visits by non-acculturated people from donor countries, and by written reports from national missionaries or their supporting national boards which are highly subjective and self-serving. These national boards sometimes have a preponderance of relatives of the director or founder on them. Consequently when the reports are produced and circulated in the West, they often paint glowing pictures of work in the field which may bear little resemblance to reality.

Integral to any meaningful biblical partnership is trust. Christian love is expressed, in part, by trusting one another in the partnership and through believing the best (1 Cor. 13:7). It is easy to grow suspicious of the 'other side' because 'they do things differently', especially if one partner (usually the Western one) is monocultural. This particularly poses problems when churches enter partnerships directly with Two-Thirds World parachurch organisations or churches. Most such churches, even if they are mega-churches, lack the cross-cultural savvy and experience to 'read' the relationship accurately. However, this direct linking with indigenous ministries is increasingly the trend and is a cause for concern. Working through the middlemen of Western-based mission agencies, both interdenominational and denominational, bypasses much potential misunderstanding or manipulation, because these agencies have the intercultural skills to obviate this sort of tension. Trust, then, is engendered as the above values are implemented.

In most global partnerships there is not usually the sort of opportunity experienced by OMers who are able to work alongside missionary colleagues from opposite sides of the world. A survey I conducted with thirty senior Indian OM leaders revealed that they had a high level of trust in their Western counterparts in OM. A number of them observed that they felt this was because a large number of the Western World leaders in OM had spent some of their early years of service with OM-India. At the time I conducted this survey, as Executive Director for OM-Canada, I met with some of the senior Indian leaders, along with leaders of many other nationalities, once a year in a gathering called the International Leaders' Meeting. At that time the German, Egyptian , Swiss, Dutch, American, *Doulos* ship, Turkish, Pakistani, Bangladeshi, and Swedish field leaders had cut their eye-teeth in missions in OM-India. Little wonder that there was a sense of camaraderie and trust in the international partnership.

Finally, biblical partnership is characterised by each partner being willing to serve the other. In seeing the other partner as better than ourselves (Phil. 2:3), and recognising that great leadership is marked by servanthood (Mk. 9:35), we overcome the tendency to ethnocentrism, and pave the way for an openness to one another's strengths in the outworking of the partnership. Empowerment, not insisting on hidden agendas being fulfilled, is the predictable feature of genuine partnerships. Such serving of the other will free Western World partners to accept Two-Thirds World strengths in the mutual relationship. Examples which immediately come to mind where non-Westerners may have strengths the self-confident Westerner needs are:

- a more holistic view of life.
- a keener sense of corporate as opposed to individual spirituality
- a simpler and more godly lifestyle
- a more vigorous prayer life and faith
- intercultural sensitivity.[17]

On the other hand, the Two-Thirds World church can tap into Western World technical expertise (although in some fields

---

[17] Such comparisons of strengths and weaknesses between the Western and Two-Thirds World are found in Bush and Lutz, *Partnering*, pp. 64–65; and Escobar, speech, 1991.

they don't really lag behind), financial resources, and theological or cross-cultural training expertise. Humility, the trademark of servanthood, esteems the assets of others objectively, without feeling threatened. Can the British church (or British parachurch agencies), for instance, accept that they have things to learn from the national Christians and the churches (some of which are massive), in the countries they formerly colonised, like Nigeria, Singapore and India?

Learning from 'The Jerusalem Relief Fund'

We see the reciprocity and mutuality of partnerships operative in the history of the early Christians in the mounting of the 'Jerusalem Relief Fund' by Paul. An examination of the dynamics of that fund-raising effort is instructive in building a theology of globalisation of missions. The first mention of Paul's fund-raising effort is found in Acts 11:27–30. There we are told that money was raised for the hard-pressed church in Judea and that the gift was sent through Paul and Barnabus. A subsequent mention of it is found in Acts 24:17 where, in the context of Paul going to Jerusalem, he was 'to bring gifts to the poor'. The material suffering of the church at Jerusalem may have been related to the persecution described in Acts 8:1, but at least we know definitely that it was the result of a severe famine in the land (Acts 11:28). Romans 15:25–31 sheds light on the documenting in Acts of this historical occurrence verifiying the fact that the church in Jerusalem was the beneficiary of the gift sent by churches in Macedonia and Achaia. 1 Corinthians 16: 3 reveals that the church at Corinth was also part of this joint venture. Galatians 2:10 verifies that it was the poor who were being ministered to.

Noteworthy in the Romans 15 passage is verse 27 because it establishes the reciprocal nature of the relationship between the largely Gentile churches giving the gift to the largely Jewish church at Jerusalem, from whom they had benefited spiritually. The Gentiles owed much of their grounding in the faith to the mother church in Jerusalem. So it is to be expected that they should be eager to return the favour, if in a different form.

Commenting on this passage, Leon Morris says, 'The money is not a soulless gift, but the outward expression of the deep love that binds Christians in one body.'[18]

But most revealing is the extensive passage in 2 Corinthians 8 and 9 where Paul's views on financial stewardship, under the inspiration of the Holy Spirit, are delineated – views which take as their application the helping of the poor in Jerusalem. Several principles interplay here in the outworking of this joint-ministry partnership. For one thing, equality is the goal in the relationship (8:13–15). Secondly, accountability is involved (8:18–21). Thirdly, there is a structure put in place for collecting and distributing the money (9:1–5). Fourthly, the relationship is grace-oriented. *Charis*, the Greek word for grace in the NT, shows up four times in the passage. Gordon Fee sums up the thrust of the passage:

> The 'collection' was not some mere matter of money, but was for Paul an active response to the grace of God that not only ministered to the needs of God's people but also became a kind of ministry to God himself, which resulted in thanksgiving toward God and in a kind of bond of fellowship between 'God's people' across the Empire.[19]

Also relevant to the proper understanding of partnership is Galatians 6:1–10. The idea of helping out the person in deep spiritual need comes through in verse 2 where believers are instructed to 'carry each other's burden and so fulfil the law of Christ.' But for such a relationship to be meaningful, it cannot be one-sided. Therefore in verse 5 a seemingly opposite principle is taught, namely, that 'each one should carry his own load.' In other words, there should be a sense of responsibility conditioning dependence on help from others in times of personal weakness. We are to bear the burdens of others, but we are also to let them bear their fair share of their own burdens. Freeloading is not encouraged here! Scripture neither teaches

---

18 Leon Morris, *The Epistle to the Romans*, Vol. 2 (Grand Rapids, MI: W.B. Eerdmans Publishing Co., 1988), p. 520.
19 Gordon Fee, *The First Epistle to the Corinthians* (Grand Rapids, MI: W.B. Eerdmans Publishing Co., 1987), p. 812.

extreme forms of individualism nor extreme forms of
communalism.

Applying this principle to the concept of partnership in missions, let's look at the frequently and hotly debated issue of
Western World financial support of nationals. Should not the
often financially-strapped church in the South, for instance,
expect the relatively wealthy church in the North to come to the
aid of the missionary activity of the church in the South? Surely
the North's response should be to ask the church in the South to
do what it can, also making real sacrifices (sacrifices by their
standards, not just the North's!), and then the North will pitch
in to make up the difference. Similarly, would it be unreason-
able to expect that a church in the South, which has been
planted among the unreached and supported from abroad,
should reach a point in time when it can be counted on to take
over full financial responsibility for paying its own pastor . . . no
longer a church planter but now a pastor?! We'll take this
subject up in more detail in chapter four.

To return to Galatians 6, verses 6 to 10 furnish us with a practical example of how partnership is to work through mutual
enabling. Congregational members in Galatia are exhorted to
provide materially for the person doing the teaching in their
midst (who is either a teaching elder or the equivalent of a
pastor). Here we have a relationship where privileges and
responsibilities apply to both parties in the partnership. One
puts the hard work into properly preparing and delivering biblical messages; the other gives material remuneration to the
preacher. Biblical partnerships should demonstrate a function-
ality whereby equality is observed through the balance of
giving and receiving on both sides of the partnership. The give
and take is genuinely operating, much like in a healthy
marriage.

THREE

God Loves Human Kinds, Not Just Humankind

Diversity in Humankind

Days after Mark McGuire broke Roger Maris' 40-year-old record of most home runs in a season, people were interviewed on TV as to what they thought about the momentous baseball event. I'll never forget one Chinese-Canadian lady. She was asked if she wanted Sammy Sosa, a Caribbean-Latin player, who was also poised to shatter the same seemingly invincible record, to end the season with more home runs than the American-born McGuire, or vice versa. She smiled and chirped, 'I hope McGuire hits the most home runs because he's an American and it's an American sport!' I thought, how magnanimous – a racial minority, enjoying racial differences for once, rather than making them the source of envy and enmity!

Just as a commitment to fostering unity in relationships is vital to a theology of globalisation in missions, so is accepting the appropriateness of diversity in relationships. Variety is enshrined in the very nature of the created order. There is tremendous diversity in the panoply of the species. When they were all created God labelled his creation as good (Gen. 1:11–24). God loves humankind and human kinds! Duane Elmer rightly contends that it is only the great variety of the human, plant, animal, and inorganic world that enables us to capture something of the grandeur, grace, and glory of God.[1]

---

[1] Duane Elmer, *Cross Cultural Conflict: Building Relationships For Effective Ministry* (Downer's Grove, IL: Inter Varsity Press, 1993), p. 24.

In Acts 17 there is the implicit acceptance of the diversity of humankind in the assertion that 'from one man he made every nation of men . . . and he determined the times set for them and the exact places where they should live' (v. 26). It is worth noting that this passage also denies the validity of pluralism in religion (vv. 27, 30–31), while upholding the legitimacy of diversity culturally and racially. So too the New Jerusalem will be enriched by the mosaic of human cultures, since 'the glory and honour of the nations will be brought into it [and] nothing impure will ever enter it' (Rev. 21:26–27a). If they will bless human life then, they can begin to do so now (cf. Rev. 7:9).[2]

Diversity is normative in the local and universal church too. Hence we find in I Corinthians 12, Paul not only exalting the unity of the Body of Christ, but also its differences, as in spiritual gifting (vv. 14–26). One of the by-products of an appreciation for the role diversity has in the life of the church is that it helps us to recognise that no one person has a monopoly on effective ministry, truth or blessing. We are accepted in Christ in the particulars of our own culture and yet we reach out to a new set of relationships which take us beyond our previously-existing world.

In summary, given that diversity exists in the church, and that the Bible validates such diversity, except where it is the result of non-conformance to biblical standards, globalisation of missions is one creative way to display the importance of this truth. It also gives us cause to wonder how right it is to press too much for homogeneous churches as an end in themselves.[3] Starting with one-culture churches may be an effective and contextualised church-planting strategy, but in the long run, if homogenous churches stay that way, can they expect to mature into all that God would have for them? Heterogeneity combined with unity (non-dominance by one faction or cultural component in the church) brings glory to God. We'll take up this subject again in chapter eight.

---

[2] Stott, *Issues* p. 207.
[3] *Homogeneous churches* are churches made up of one racial or socio-economic group, for example.

The Importance of Community

The aforementioned principles of globalisation can be seen in one sense to stem from the character of God Himself. Not surprisingly then, we see in the Godhead the principle of community at work too. The persons of the Trinity dwell in individuality and yet in relationship with each other (Jn. 10:40; 14:16–23). Therefore, it is to be expected that we see God fashioning a companion for Adam (Gen. 2:18). Part of what it means to be made in the image of God is to experience completeness in the relationship between a male and a female (Gen. 1:27). Throughout the history of the Israelites and the church, we are brought back to this fundamental truth: God exhibits His Kingdom on earth most authentically in the context of real relationships (Mt. 18:20; 1 Kgs. 8:11). This is a biblical theme which encourages us to be proponents of whatever it takes to be in healthy community with other believers (Gal. 6:10). Global partnership is but one more Kingdom expression of community. Unfortunately the individualism of the West has resulted in the loss of a genuine sense of community among God's people.[4]

The NT word *oikoumene* captures effectively what we are driving at here. An important aspect of globalisation is being in community. In its fourteen usages in the NT, *oikoumene* always refers to the inhabited world in the expansive sense.[5] This kind of worldwide sense of the term is found, for example, in Acts 17:31: 'For he has set a day when he will judge the world with justice by the man he has appointed.' The word translated as *world* is *oikoumene*. In this same passage God is pictured as being the Father of us all. The brotherhood of man is more than just an idle expression. In a very real sense, we are all in the same boat of humanity. The whole of humanity in itself forms a community and so provides a basis for promoting globalisation. My worldwide travels and living have repeatedly driven home to me the point that in one sense

---

[4] Phillip Butler, 'Kingdom Partnerships in the 90s: Is there a New Way Forward?' in Taylor, *Kingdom Partnerships* 1994, pp. 15–17.
[5] Arndt and Gringrich, *Lexicon*, p. 561.

people are the same everywhere. I've seen Afghans in the Hindu Kush mountains worry over how they were going to survive a brutal winter in the same way as a Canadian single-parent mom worried over how to cope on a meagre income with a household of kids. I've seen a Hindu wedding in Delhi celebrated with the same joy and exuberance as a Christian wedding in Toronto. Globalisation simply acknowledges our close affinity with each other in the human race. Rather than focusing on our differences, it concentrates on our similarities. We are essentially the same. We should not pull away from attempts at globalisation for fear, for instance, of paving the way for one world government! The global village concept is not an eschatological conspiracy but a social reality which inspires us to work more closely across cultures, irrespective of national borders.

The Principle of the Dignity of Work

Another major area which needs fleshing out in order to fashion a proper theology of globalisation relates to the age-old question of self-reliance versus acceptance of charity. In the history of missions, this issue has surfaced repeatedly. In more recent centuries it has crystallised in the debate which has come to be characterised as the 'Three-Self Movement'. The Three-Self Movement refers to a philosophy of mission which promotes the indigenisation of the emerging church in the Two-Thirds World. The three selves of self-governing, self-propagating, and self-financing are viewed as indices of a church becoming indigenised, that is, being able to stand on its own two feet without outside missionary support. American, Rufus Anderson, and Briton, Henry Venn, were the primary spokesmen for this philosophy of missions which became popular almost a century ago and which has found favour in mission circles until recently. It is the contention here that three aspects of the issue need to be addressed thoughtfully in order for biblical balance to be achieved, but no more than a skeletal consideration will be proffered at this juncture. These aspects are: the importance of the work ethic, the right to earn one's living by the Gospel, and the need for equability in the distribution of the church's limited material resources.

First of all, Scripture is clear about the responsibility of all believers to work for their own living (1 Tim. 5:8; Gal. 6:4–5). Any theology of creation must acknowledge work as being inherent in the stewardship of the earth as placed in man's and woman's hands (Gen. 1:26, 28–30; Ps. 8:6). II Thessalonians 3:10 goes so far as to say that if a person does not work, he or she should not eat. This exhortation comes in the context of Paul dealing with busybodies and of pointing to his own model of a proper work ethic as he makes tents in their midst (vv. 6–9; Acts 18:3; 1 Cor. 4:12). Thus in Paul's emphasis on work, there is an encouraging of self-support.[6] In Proverbs there is an invaluable perspective on the causes of poverty, among which is a lack of industriousness (Prov. 6:10; 13:18; 13:4). Much material blessing is said to be a result of God's grace to his children (Prov. 8:12–21), but elsewhere Scripture stresses the place of human responsibility in the matter. Beyerhaus makes the point that Paul's churches were self-supporting and that the concept of the full-time, salaried pastor, so common in the twentieth century, did not enter church thinking until the fifth century.[7] Nevertheless, pastors like Timothy did seem to depend on their churches for their remuneration. At the very least, caution must be exercised where any segment of the global church seems to be absolving itself of its own monetary responsibility in its efforts to fulfil the Great Commission. In intercultural joint ventures, then, there ought to be a commitment to shoulder a significant proportion of the financial burden by both partners, lest any unhealthy dependence emerge.

Secondly, to balance the above principle, Scripture also teaches that those who are engaged exclusively in direct ministry have the right to be paid for services rendered. One such reference is I Corinthians 9:7–14 (see also Gal. 6:10). I Timothy 5:17 goes a step further in saying that such ministers of the Gospel should be remunerated generously! An attitude that too

---

[6] R. J. Sims, *Wealth and Poverty, Self-Support and Sharing in the Church Worldwide: A Biblical Study With Missiological Implication* (M.A. thesis, Fuller Theological Seminary, 1989), p. 218.
[7] Beyerhaus, *Shaken Foundations*, 1964, pp. 401–402.

often permeates churches, unfortunately, is that so-called 'full-time' Christian workers, especially if they are missionaries, are morally bound to make sacrifices that the 'normal' Christian population does not have to make. But the cross-cultural missionary needs a sense of emotional well-being in his or her work. Given the way God has created us, to deny a person material well-being, is to subject the average missionary to a distraction from single-minded ministry. Financial pressures are cited as a typical reason for the 40 per cent attrition rate of missionaries not lasting more than one term on the field. That is not to say that Western missionaries' affluent lifestyle, in comparison with their Two-Thirds World counterparts, is not a cause of alienation from the very people they have crossed the seas to reach, as Jon Bonk so painstakingly (and painfully!) documents in his ground-breaking book *Missions and Money*. However, let it not be assumed that the under-financing of missionary work is a uniquely Western problem. Documentors of the rise of the Two-Thirds World missionary movement have been quick to point out that Two-Thirds World missionaries, in spite of their reduced material expectations and demands, are often languishing on the field under-provided for.[8] Indian Missions Association, for one, is addressing this issue by seeking to set standards for salaries for Indian missionaries, and by seeking out assistance from Indian churches in helping underwrite undersupported missionaries.[9] In such cases, is it not the moral obligation of the more prosperous sectors of the global church to respond somewhat to the needs of under-funded national mission agencies?

Harvey Conn makes the insightful observation that the Pauline pattern in I Corinthians 9: 14 is to receive support from the church for which one labours and therefore that we are teaching emerging churches the wrong thing when we (outsiders) pay the missionary or national pastor to work in their midst.

---

[8] Luis Bush, *Funding Third World Missions* (Wheaton, IL: World Evangelical Fellowship Missions Committee, 1990), p. 26; Larry Keyes, *The Last Age of Missions* (Pasadena, CA: William Carey Library, 1983), pp. 115–116.

[9] They estimate that half of the national missionaries associated with them are undersupported. This programme is described in 'Cell For Assistance and Relief To Evangelists,' *Indian Missions*. Jan.-Mar., 1997, pp. 20–23.

Thus we short-circuit the national church in seeing that it has a responsibility not only to care for the needs of its national pastor but to some extent, if largely symbolically, those of its foreign missionary.[10]

Thirdly, equability of distribution of limited resources should be in view in globalisation of missions. What do we mean by equability? The term equability is used instead of equality because the issue is not uniformity of treatment but fairness of treatment. For example, it would be ludicrous to raise a Bangladeshi missionary's standard of living to a British missionary colleague's middle-class standard just because equality of salary is being sought. In the Bangladeshi community's eyes, the Bangladeshi missionary's new standard of living would elevate him to the level of a maharaja! But it would be fair to raise his salary to the level of the Bangladeshi middle class and reduce the Englishman's salary so as to make it consistent with that of the Bangladeshi upper-middle-class level. That way the expatriate doesn't have to make too painful an adjustment nor is the national alienating himself from the people he is trying to reach. This is a delicate area where there are no easy answers, but a more contextualised approach to establishing lifestyles for missionaries in multi and intercultural teams ought to be undertaken.

Scripture is clear that God hates economic oppression and injustice (Deut. 15:1–11; Jer. 22:25–29; Is. 5:22–23; Prov. 13:23; Jas. 1:27; 2:5–9; 1 Jn. 3:17–18). The antithesis of such oppression and injustice is not benign neglect, but the intentionalised assistance of poverty-stricken and vulnerable people, as underscored in the parable of the Good Samaritan. Those well-off are to help the less fortunate (as we saw in the examination of the outworking of the 'Jerusalem Relief Fund'). To extrapolate from this principle, then, it makes sense to expect that the Western World church will take seriously its opportunity to help finance agencies or churches involved in penetrating unreached people groups from the Two-Thirds World with the Gospel – at least where demonstrable financial need exists. Of

---

[10] Harvey Conn, 'The Money Barrier Between Sending and Receiving Churches,' *Evangelical Missions Quarterly* 14(4) (October, 1978): 233, 235.

course it is important not to generalise. Increasingly, certain elements of the Two-Thirds World church, such as Korea, Malaysia, and Singapore, are not at all interested in accessing Western World financial partnerships: they are demonstrating an ability and willingness to shoulder their own fiscal burdens. In fact, the Korean church in particular is establishing a track record of generously providing for the needs of its own missionaries in cross-cultural ministry.[11]

Sims sums up well the issues involved in seeking to redress economic inequalities which are glaringly obvious to many as they survey the missions' scene today:

> The day must soon come when leaving the mission churches' pastors, evangelists, and catechists in abject poverty will be recognised for what it is – a travesty of God's revelation that such dehumanizing poverty is contrary to his will. God speed the day when such a phenomenon will be as unacceptable as slavery. If such servants of God are left in poverty because of the application of self-support, then the principle has been misapplied. God never intended his servants to be degraded in such a manner, especially while within the worldwide church there are resources available for their proper maintenance.[12]

These then are the principles which form a biblical theology of the globalisation of missions: the unity of humankind, and of the church; partnership in ministry; the diversity of humankind and of the church; the community of humankind and of the church, and equability in the sharing of resources in the context of responsible stewardship in mission partnerships.

---

[11] This self-support has become more problematic recently with the devaluation of the Korean currency worldwide.
[12] Sims, *Wealth and Poverty*, p. 239.

FOUR

Whither Blows the Wind?

Is it inevitable that the church and missions get swept up in the worldwide trend toward globalisation? To answer that question we need to come to grips with the pervasiveness of globalisation in the world in general. Why is it happening? What form does it take? How extensive is it? Having considered such questions, we still want to know if globalisation of missions is a healthy development. In a sense, we have already addressed the question of whether globalisation of missions is a good thing, by exploring a theological apologetic for it in the previous two chapters. So we might say that, all things being equal, we don't want to halt globalisation of missions in its tracks, but we may discover some reservations along the way.

Nevertheless, we must not accept uncritically what the world and culture throw at us. Culture intersects biblical truth at every turn. As Christians, our job is to live relevantly in the world without compromising truth or the Gospel, without allowing the world to squeeze us into its mold. Therefore, before we can jump on the bandwagon of globalisation, we need to understand what it is really fashioning in our world and where it is taking us, critiquing it carefully and thoughtfully.

The World of Communications

Perhaps no field of endeavour has sped us quicker toward globalisation than communications. As far back as 1970, people like futurist Alvin Toffler in *Future Shock*, were forecasting revolutionary ways we would perceive our world as a result of the introduction of technology like the computer. Modern communications' technology has enabled people to transcend national boundaries in ways not dreamed of less than a generation ago. This new reality was no more vividly illustrated for us than in the tragedy of Tinananmen Square. As the Chinese army sought to clamp down forcibly on the growing movement among students towards liberalisation and democratisation, the government censored the protesters' contact with the outside world. But from the centre of Beijing, where the students were congregating in revolutionary dissent, the outside world continued to monitor developments. How? Through the students who were conveying up-to-date reports of the unfolding events by fax machine! Transmitting information instantaneously, the facsimile allowed distant recipients to react immediately, vicariously, or even in influential terms, with remote events.

Telecommunications are fashioning a global village which will make the world of tomorrow even more unrecognisable to us than today's world is for our grandparents, many of whom lived through the introduction of the telephone, the radio, and the television. Modern telecommunications include consumer electronics, televisions, telephones, and computers. The promised marvel of the Internet is but one example of a blending of the strengths of differing technologies. The Internet simply marries the technologies of the telephone and the computer in a way which empowers individuals, through heightening their ability to communicate with each other, to bypass national borders, company boundaries, and group restraints. It is estimated that there are now over four hundred million individuals using the Internet and that that number will soon reach one and a quarter billion. As a result, while these technologies are enabling corporations to develop world markets and international presence, they are shifting power to small businesses and specialised groups who have the same information and access to markets that the big players have. A personal computer in a home office now has the capability of a microcomputer of a decade ago. John Naisbitt predicts in *Global*

Paradox that 'the telecommunications business will double and redouble as we drive toward global interconnectivity.'[1]

Then there is television. Until several years ago, the only television you could view in India was the dreary, government-run TV network. It symbolised an India which remained very traditional, a parochial society, in spite of its sophistication scientifically and in other ways. But then satellite TV was introduced to India. Within a matter of months, India became globally conscious as it had never been before. Indian men now followed baseball avidly, when before only cricket was known as the game where you swung a bat. After all, when you tune into the BBC News channel or the TSN Sports channel there is more to watch than Hindi melodramas! Teenagers wear Michael Jackson T-shirts as readily as they do the embroidered kurtas. A recent Michael Jackson album sold fifteen million copies, two-thirds of those outside the United States, many of them in India. Imported shows like *Baywatch* paint a view of the Western world which reshapes moral and cultural values unenvisaged a few years ago.

This story can be repeated all over the world. It's called the 'Hollywoodisation' (read mainly Americanisation) of culture. The French want a Walt Disney theme park. Taiwanese read *The Economist*. Everyone 'cool' drinks Coca-Cola, listens to Alanis Morissette on CD, and watches Arnold Schwarzenegger action movies on their VCRs. A consumer outlook and materialistic expectations cut across cultures. Borders become redundant. Totalitarian regimes, like Cuba's, increasingly become anachronisms, in the face of this globalising tide. The world is becoming incredibly interconnected. As Naisbitt puts it, 'The telecommunications revolution . . . create[s] a seamless, global . . . network of networks that will allow everyone in the world to be connected with everyone else.'[2]

One telecommunications innovation due to reach the market place within the next two decades will shrink our globe even more. It is a wireless video phone hooked to a notebook computer which will recognise handwriting and the spoken word.

---

[1] John Naisbitt, *Global Paradox* (New York: Avon Books, 1994), p. 61.
[2] *Ibid.*, p. 62.

This 'personal assistant' will have the ability to translate the spoken word into another language, as designated by the speaker. Such an 'automatic interpreting telephone', as engineers call it, will enable one to converse with someone on the other side of the world so that the conversation is two-way and whereby you can see the one to whom you are talking.[3] What a way to reduce language and geographical barriers! Other inventions will similarly alter the way we think about people different from ourselves, do work, make money, and embrace values.

Leadership and Management Strategy

Quite possibly the word *globalisation* is found most frequently in management literature. Doing a quick survey of some of that literature will help us to understand the nuances and meanings of *globalisation*. Some crossover between the way terms are used creates a certain amount of confusion, but also helps to clarify meanings as the literature is analysed. Hofstede, for example, distinguishes between *multinational* and *international* when describing companies that work in more than one country.[4] A *multinational corporation*, he says, is one like IBM which has business relations in many countries but which has a dominant home culture to which most pivotal decision makers belong. On the other hand, an *international corporation* is one like the United Nations which has key decision makers coming from member nations. Hofstede does not use the word *globalisation* but it is evident that he would view the UN as the more globalised organisation of the two, using our working definition as the basis for measurement.

A more refined classification is developed by Craig.[5] He describes three types of international companies:

An *ethnocentric organisation* is a complex organisation in a home country with centralised decision making in the

---

[3] *Ibid.*, pp. 75–76.
[4] Cited in P. R. Harris and R. T. Moran, *Managing Cultural Differences* (Houston: Gulf Publishing, 1987), p. 246.
[5] Cited in *ibid.*, pp. 15–16.

headquarters there. Evaluation and control are based on home standards, and communication flows outward to subsidiaries in host countries with ownership and recruitment of crucial management largely coming from the home country.

A *polycentric organisation* has less authority and decision making from headquarters, with evaluation done locally. Ownership, key management, and recruitment are from the host nation.

A *geocentric organisation* is an increasingly complex, interdependent organisation which seeks collaboration between and among headquarters/subsidiaries. It uses standards for evaluation and control which are at times universal, and at times local. Ownership, key management, and recruitment are global. Obviously, the latter of these three organisations is the most sophisticatedly globalised.

Moran, an intercultural management consultant, even more helpfully understands this graduated approach to the sort of organisational complexity that can be called globalised.[6] He uses four differentiations instead of Craig's three, with the *polycentric organisation* being divided into European (*multinational structure*) and American (*international structure*) versions of it. It is interesting to note that he calls the final stage of organisational development – *global structure*. Such an organisation has a strong international headquarters, with firm central control, distributes resources without regarding country of origin, and cultivates the world as its marketplace.

A common thread throughout the analysis of these management specialists is that they do not see globalisation as undermining the integrity of localisation or regionalisation. Consultants advising multinational corporations, like Toffler, similarly are saying that globalisation does not necessarily undercut initiative and vibrancy at the local level. And so Toffler argues convincingly as follows:

> Globalization . . . is not the same as homogenity. Instead of a single global village, as forecast by Marshall McLuhan, the late Canadian media theorist, we are likely

---

[6] R. T. Moran. 'Making Globalization Work,' *World Executive's Digest*. January, 1993, p. 16.

to see a multiplicity of quite different global villages – all wired into the media system, but all straining to retain or enhance their cultural, ethnic, national, or political individuality.[7]

Naisbitt similarly argues that, paradoxically, the realities of universalisation and *tribalisation* will not work at cross-purposes in the world of the future. As he says, 'In one of the major turnarounds in my lifetime, we have moved from the "economies of scale" to "diseconomies of scale"; from bigger is better to bigger is inefficient, costly, wastefully bureaucratic, inflexible, and now, disastrous.'[8] Faith Popcorn calls this distaste and distrust of 'bigness' – *icon toppling*. It is one of the sixteen future trends identified in her recent best-seller, *Clicking*.

Toffler calls corporations which have this global reach *mega-firms*.[9] Six hundred such firms account for one-fifth of the value of agricultural and industrial production in the world.[10] Toffler cites Visa International as an example of a 'nationless' corporation in that although it has its international headquarters in the United States, it is owned by twenty-one thousand institutions in 187 countries. Its governing and regional boards are set up to prevent any one country from having 51 per cent of the vote.[11]

Other words used to distinguish between more localised or regionalised firms versus far-reaching international ones, include Kvin calling the latter *multinational*.[12] However, the most frequently used word to describe the far-reaching ones is *global*, Kenai Ohmae being one of the better known intercultural management experts who uses this term in his ongoing analysis of the place of Japan on the world market scene.[13]

---

[7] Alvin Toffler, *Power Shift: Knowledge, Wealth and Violence at the Edge of the Twenty-First Century* (Toronto: Bantam Books, 1990), p. 341.

[8] Naisbitt, *Global Paradox* pp. 12–13.

[9] *Ibid.*, p. 460.

[10] *Ibid.*

[11] *Ibid.*

[12] P. Kvin, 'The Magic of Multinational Management,' *Harvard Business Review*. (November-December, 1972): 97.

[13] In addition to the aforementioned Harris and Moran using *globalisation* to describe such companies, see also K. Ohmae, *The Borderless World* (New York: Harper Business, 1990); K. Ohmae, *Triad Power: The Coming Shape of Global*

On the other hand, there is the fear in the West, as borders collapse in the face of a growing global economy, that jobs will be lost in the West. For example, headlining a recent Business section of the *Toronto Star* was the story of how Bell Canada, one of the country's largest companies, was shipping millions of dollars of computer work offshore, to India, where labour is far cheaper. Bell put its contract out to tender and chose the best package to convert paper maps and diagrams of its vast network of cable, wires and poles into computer format. Part of that package included transferring the majority of the work – the data conversion of 500,000 maps into digital form-to India. This is no accident because India, especially in the Bangalore area, has one of the world's largest and best-performing software programming work forces.

Pulling these various strands of management literature together is not too difficult. Globalisation, although not always called such, is seen as the most advanced form of international corporate structuring. Different terms are used to delineate the different stages of the evolutionary process from regional to universal influence and mindset. A clear distinction is made between the universalising qualities of globalisation in business and the protection of localised heterogeneity. Strengths of local branches or subsidiaries are respected and guarded, unlike in the earlier stages of corporate development where ethnocentrism reigns supreme.

The World of Economics

Related, naturally, to management thinking on globalisation, are the trends on the world economic scene. Over the last decade or so the global economy has shifted away from being powered by political ideologies to economic pragmatism. National products, companies and industries are giving way to leading-edge transnational conglomerates whose organisational charts look

---

[13] *(continued) Competition* (New York: The Free Press, 1985); John Naisbitt. 'Globalized Education,' *Inside Guide*. Summer, 1990, pp. 8–9; and M. Schrage. 'A Japanese Giant Rethinks Globalization: An Interview With Yoshihisa Tabuchi,' *Harvard Business Review*. (July – August, 1989): 70–76.

like spider webs rather than pyramids. The earth's economy is decreasingly dominated by multinationals which are distinctly European, American, or Japanese. Tourism is the world's largest business and employer. National boundaries are disregarded in the search for more qualified research scientists, software engineers, consultants, information managers, teachers, investment bankers, and design engineers. The upshot of these global economic changes is a levelling of national idiosyncrasies and a paradigm shift in thinking so as to project in global rather than parochial terms. Global economic integration is like a corrosive acid eating away at the sovereignty of nations.

A startling observation is made by John Naisbitt in his book, *Megatrends Asia*. He argues in it that the third most powerful economy in the world is the fifty-seven million 'Overseas Chinese', that is, those who live outside China but who have forged interconnecting links that defy nation-state borders.[14] The Overseas Chinese have now outranked Germany and other European nations as a world-leading economy, and are only overshadowed by the economies of the United States and Japan. We have only become aware of them in Canada in recent years, even though they have been present for more than a generation. Real estate values have soared in Toronto and Vancouver not only because of the new-found wealth of the well-educated and hard-working resident Chinese, but because of new money coming from offshore Chinese, particularly those from Hong Kong. In East Asia, the Overseas Chinese dominate nation economies in every country except Korea and Japan. Bound by family, social, and business ties, many Chinese networks facilitate their own agendas and welfare across national lines. They are an example of new economic paradigms which have global dimensions. Similarly, the non-resident Indian population worldwide is large. Ten million of them outside India control an estimated income of $340 billion.[15] Some of that pours back into India.

---

[14] John Naisbitt, *Megatrends Asia* (New York: Simon & Shuster Inc., 1996), pp. 17–23.
[15] *Ibid.*, pp. 48–49.

Asian economies are booming to the extent that some fore-casters are saying that in order for Western companies to remain competitive on the world scene they will have to do a growing amount of business in Asia. And why wouldn't they want to expand into these burgeoning new markets? Asian economies have grown six to ten per cent in the last decade. This is creating a massive middle class which could number one billion people by the year 2010, triggering up to $10 trillion in spending power.[16] While it took a century for Great Britain's middle class to emerge, almost overnight India has a middle class of one hundred to two hundred million people.[17] And they all want CDs, VCRs, and designer jeans! If this sort of thing won't make the world a global village, what will?!

When I first went to India in the early seventies, refrigerators were often put in the living or dining room. They were a status symbol of new-found wealth. Not anymore. They're more likely to be in the kitchen. Now it's the TV and the VCR that are put in the living room. Downtown Bombay is full of stores that are as sophisticated and chic as Harrods. The world has shrunk because the Two-Thirds World economies are now consumer driven. They want what Western nations have been privy to for generations – an affluent life style, and that means a continued fascination with the West even as they distance themselves philosophically in other respects.

The World of Missions

One final field or world we would like to peek into to deter-mine how globalisation is being understood and impacting is

---

[16] *Ibid.*, p. 89.

[17] However, what is being referred to as the booming Chinese and Indian middle classes must be kept in perspective. In their article 'The End of Corporate Imperialism' in *Harvard Business Review*, C. K. Prahalad and Kenneth Lieberthal point out that only 2 per cent of the population in China and 7 per cent in India have the purchasing power in US$ comparable to Western World middle classes, that is, with greater than $20,000 per annum purchasing power (Vol. 76, No. 4, July – August, 1998, p. 71).

missions.[18] This field needs to be divided into two. Missiologists (those who study the science and theology of missions) have taken an approach similar to other theologians whereas missionaries and other mission leaders (the practitioners of the theory) often seem to have a different emphasis. Missiologist Thomas, for one, has written specifically on the subject of globalisation of missions.[19] For him, globalisation embraces things in everyday life which demonstrate the interconnectedness of the world: threats to survival from human conflict, technical innovations enhancing global communication, and policies threatening global ecology. A missiologist in the classroom, therefore, in this view, serves as a catalyst in fostering a paradigm shift from parochialism to universalism when he or she seeks to bring about globalisation.

Going along with Thomas' emphasis is Jon Bonk's article entitled 'Globalization and Mission Education'. His perspective is that globalisation is more an attitude of overcoming Western triumphalism and provincialism than a quantifiable entity. And so we find him philosophising that, 'perhaps globalisation is, after all, more of a direction than a destination [involving a] repenting of parochialism.'[20]

Samuel Escobar epitomises globalisation in that he is thoroughly Latin American and yet has spent over two decades providing parachurch and missiological leadership in North America. So we need to listen closely to what he has to say about the matter. He clarifies the term *internationalisation*, identifying it as primarily involving partnership between East and West (or North and South) in the task of doing mission, a partnership affecting leadership, relationships, and styles of

---

[18] We distinguish here between *missions* and *mission*. *Mission* is the calling of the church to make disciples of all nations, as embodied in the Great Commission. *Missions* is the church reaching out with the Gospel where there is no church. *Evangelism* is the church reaching out where the church is. I am indebted to Dr. Ralph Winter for this simple yet profound distinction. Both *evangelism* and *missions* are encompassed in fulfilling the *mission* of the church. David Bosch also has a helpful discussion of the use of the terms in *Transforming Mission* (Maryknoll, NY: Orbis Books, 1996), p. 1.

[19] N. E. Thomas, 'Globalization and the Teaching of Mission,' *Missiology: An International Review* 18(1) (January, 1990): 13–23.

[20] Jon Bonk, 'Globalization and Mission Education,' *Theological Education* 30(1) (Autumn, 1993): 75.

operating.[21] Padilla and Hendricks do use the word *globalisation*, and without defining it clearly, associate it with a worldwide perspective, and partnership of the church in mission as equals between East and West.[22]

Mission leaders – practitioners of missions – have not been remiss in focusing on globalisation. However, their tendency has been to call it *partnership* or *internationalisation*. William Taylor is at the forefront of a move towards more globalisation in missions, through organising consultations on the subject and editing two books dealing with globalisation issues. In one of these books he seems to be reaching for the distinction between *globalisation* and *internationalisation* when he differentiates between 'staff internationalization of mission agencies' (called *internationalisation* herein) and 'internationalization of the missionary movement' (called herein *globalisation*). He uses Peter Hamm's definition of *globalisation* to refer to the 'transcending of national boundaries, not only in reaching the goal of our mandate, but in the processes of planning, organising and implementing the mandate.'[23]

David Hicks, one of OM's top international leaders, introduced the concept of globalisation to OM which has been adopted into our official statement on globalisation and identified as one of seven key areas where we need to concentrate efforts organisationally as we move towards the year AD 2000. Although rightly assuming (according to the position taken here) that 'internationalization . . . is only the starting point for globalization', Hicks seems to blur his distinction somewhat by offering prima facie that globalisation 'is the process by which organizations move beyond merely operating internationally from a single or dominant national base to operating transnationally, not tied to any particular country or region.'[24] The qualifying statement to his definition of globalisation seems to be more in line with the narrow end of the funnel that

[21] Escobar. Speech, 1991.
[22] Rene Padilla and B. Hendricks, 'Mission in the 1990s: Two Views,' *International Bulletin of Missionary Research* 13(4) (1989): 146–152.
[23] Hamm, *EMQ* p. 180.
[24] Operation Mobilisation, *OM's Book of Standard Definitions* (Carlisle, England: OM Books, 1994), p. 13.

we characterise globalisation to be: 'Globalization in mission involves not only carrying out ministry across cultures [which his first statement implies], but also accomplishing the resourcing, governing, planning, and organizing of missions by involving the church in diverse regions of our planet.'[25]

The word *transnational* seems to be what is being qualified in the second statement, which significantly puts the stress on the transcending of national limitations. But one is left with the impression that externals (international involvement in recruiting, financing, and presence at decision-making levels) is what matters in measuring globalisation. As we shall see later, the internals of embracing non-western styles of thinking, interacting, values, etc., which help fashion organisational culture, are not taken into account adequately. This surface or easily quantifiable view of globalisation is commonly held in mission circles.

Popular among mission leaders is the term *equal partnership* to denote globalisation.[26] Again it is the way that the church in the Western World relates to the church in the Two-Thirds World in the task of world evangelisation that is in view here.[27]

After integrating the various senses in which globalisation or its equivalents are used in missions it can be concluded that: it has to do with an attitude fostering universals as opposed to ethnocentrism in all aspects of doing mission; it concerns the process of moving from an embryonic stage of being international within mission agencies, or in joint ventures between Western and Two-Thirds World segments of the church, to a pervasive level of internationality; and it relates to the specifics, the pragmatics of the joint mission.

Common Ground

Synthesising the ways in which the term *globalisation* is used inter-disciplinarily, and observing ways it is emerging in

---

[25] *Ibid.*

[26] E.g., Paul Pierson in Patrick Sookhdeo, *New Frontiers in Mission* (Australia: Paternoster Press, 1987), p. 10 and Luis Bush, *Funding* 1990), p. 30.

[27] For a fuller documentation of the way the term *partnership* is used by missio[n] leaders see chapter two in the section on partnership.

current events, may help us arrive at a better understanding of what globalisation really means. This is an important step in determining how we in the church should respond to the phenomenon of globalisation of missions – our primary concern in this book. What is common ground among the fields surveyed, is the cultivation of a paradigm shift in thinking and activity so that parochialism, paternalism, nationalism, and ethnocentrism give way to universals, and the complementary strengths of those unlike us. Perhaps in an earlier day we would consider *globalisation* to be a synonym for *world evangelisation* or *missions*. However, that is a given – a metonymy, since the term *mission* in itself encompasses the global dimensions of evangelising (Mt. 28:18–20). We hardly need another term to simply describe what we have already been hard at work doing for over two hundred years, and quite comfortably calling *missions*. No, the Holy Spirit is up to something more than reminding us in new language of what our calling is as the church! He is enabling the whole church to reach the whole world for Christ in a common front.

The global mindset is always functional, and so globalisation will be expressed in some form of practical partnership affecting areas like governance, financial responsibility, organisational culture, and the drawing on of the strengths of the diverse sides of the group. So for example, a church in Manchester may provide regular financial support and fervent, informed prayer for a Nigerian missionary involved in a cross-cultural church plant in Mombasa, Kenya. But the global mindset is also subtler. Globalisation of missions will need to be demonstrated in the hidden areas of how to view authority figures, how to use time, how to relate to the opposite sex, how to express feelings in the group context, and how to resolve interpersonal conflict in intercultural situations. Intra-mission values currently favour Western World missionaries. Will that change? A mission cannot call itself globalised until its Two-Thirds World missionaries feel at home in their own organisation.

FIVE

Partnership or Opportunism?

When the OM ship, *Doulos*, tied up to its berth in Santos, Brazil, back in 1981, little did its missionary and marine crew realise it would be birthing a far-reaching ministry to drug addicts. The port area of this Latin city was right in the thick of the red-light district. As always the ship staff and local Christians, volunteering to work with the ship, saturated the surrounding area inviting people to visit this marine United Nations, with over twenty-five nationalities on board and home to the largest floating book exhibition in the world. One of those who received an invitation was Padora, a heroin addict and pusher with a police record.[1]

Padora decided to pay a visit to the *Doulos*. He had nothing better to do. While he was on board, looking at the book exhibition held on the stern, he heard of a programme about to begin in the lounge and so decided to attend. He did not expect the heavy-duty impact the film, *Shiokari Pass*, shown in the meeting, would have on him. Faced with the challenge to turn his life over to Jesus Christ, Padora did so and walked off the ship a changed man.

Some years later an OM worker visiting Brazil learned of Padora's story. After being turned on to 'pushing Jesus' through his contact with the Gospel ship, this former drug addict, Padora, had spent a year in Peru in training and working with other drug addicts. Padora had then returned home to start a church, in an area reputed to be the AIDS capital of South

---

[1]   This story comes from the reporting of Debbie Meroff, who works out of OM's international headquarters in England.

America. The church in Santos now has between four and five hundred members and carries on an effective outreach to addicts and prostitutes.

Can nationals do the job? You bet they can! Like Padora has! And here's the catch. They can do it for ten times less the cost, in many cases! At least that's the claim of mission agencies whose sole objective is to facilitate the ministry of national missionaries. Consider this advert appearing in a Christian Aid Mission magazine.[2] There is a striking photograph of an Indian evangelist clutching a Bible in one hand and a lantern in the other. The caption reads: 'IMAGINE A PIONEER MISSIONARY TO UNREACHED PEOPLES WHO LIVES ON $30.00 PER MONTH, FULL SUPPORT.' This mission claims that the average support needed by two hundred thousand Two-Thirds World nationals it is helping through five thousand indigenous missions is $30.00 per month.[3] Similarly the argument is commonly heard that it cost ten times as much to field a Westerner than a national as a missionary, so why continue to support foreign missionaries from the West? Just send us your hard-earned pounds or dollars and we will invest them more wisely for you! But is this sort of claim partnership or opportunism? In this chapter we want to address the financial side of globalisation as it relates to world evangelisation, particularly in the support of nationals. Part of the driving force behind the writing of this book was a desire to seek to bring greater balance to the relatively unchallenged trend of supporting national missionaries.

The fact of the matter is that it is cheaper to field a national missionary than a Westerner. However, there are exceptions. For instance, if the Two-Thirds World missionary is working in the West, it is naive to think that it is going to cost any less to house, feed, and provide living expenses for a family of four

---

[2] Christian Aid Mission is an organisation working exclusively on behalf of national missions and missionaries. The advert in question comes from a 1993 edition of their magazine.

[3] In interviews I conducted with the Canadian Directors of Gospel For Asia (Wendell Latham on November 25, 1994) and Partners International (Grover Crosby on November 18, 1994) they repudiated this low dollar figure. Christian Aid Mission may have increased their figure since the publishing of this report.

nationals than for a Western family. A good example of this would be an OM missionary family, Chacko and Radha Thomas, currently working with OM's international head-quarters' team in London, England. When the Thomases moved from the ship, *Logos II* (which normally ministers in Latin America or Asia) to England, their missionary support requirements doubled.

As Latins, Africans, and Asians are sent out from their mis-sion-minded home churches to the unreached world, they will discover what their British, German, Danish and American pre-decessors discovered: 'Missions ain't cheap!'. Furthermore, when you shift from single to married status, to married-with-children, life gets more complicated. In 1971, when I started out in missions, albeit as a short-term missionary, all I needed to raise was $500.00 support per month. Today a fam-ily of four typically will need $4500 support per month (£2000) to serve cross-culturally in long-term work.

When all is said and done, disregarding the exceptions, and assuming national missionaries have on average two children, their support needs working in a culturally and economically-similar context to their homeland (e.g., moving from Nigeria to Morocco, or from south India to north India) will be qualita-tively different from those of Canadians or Swedes going to the same places. The $30.00 per month may swell to $400.00 per month, but who's counting when you are not talking thou-sands? Let's admit that the organisations specialising in the support of nationals have a point. Let's not strain at gnats and swallow camels! It *is* considerably cheaper to field a national missionary rather than a Westerner—even if you are talking about 'expensive lifestyle' examples of nationals and 'simple lifestyle' examples of Westerners.

Some of the differences in support levels can be attributed to unavoidable factors. Since most of the unreached world lies in the 10/40 Window of North Africa, the Middle East, and Cen-tral and South Asia, costly international flights to and from the field of service face the Westerner.[4] On the other hand, to fly

---

[4] The term '10/40 Window' refers to the region of the world bounded by west Africa to East Asia, from ten degrees north latitude to forty degrees north lati-tude. In it are found 97 per cent of people who live in the least evangelised nations.

from Uzbekistan to Singapore while on furlough will not be as expensive for a Chinese missionary. In the East, families are expected to care for their aged loved ones, so the safety net of a pension plan does not need to be built into the support structure of the Two-Thirds Worlder. Some differences are related to lower lifestyle expectations in comparison with Westerners. The missionary from the West may very well expect a refrigerator, and other appliances, along with car, which would still be considered as luxuries in many Asian church planting settings. Asian missionaries are used to the bacterias and viruses of Asia and therefore may not need the same medical protection and treatment as their Western counterparts. The differences go on and on.

Therefore it is not surprising that one of the newest trends in thinking, going on in churches in the West today, is the shifting of financial support from Westerners to nationals from the Two-Thirds World. The church I pastor adopted into its missionary budget the regular monthly support of a first such national in 1996, with a second added in 1997. Our last two missions' conferences have focused on the rise of the Two-Thirds World missionary force.

With the Two-Thirds World church emerging as a major player on the world missions scene, as chronicled in chapter one, arriving at a theologically-sound and pragmatically-balanced stance on this complicated topic is imperative. To help us know where to plant our feet, let me list several negatives and several positives for making a paradigm shift toward support of national missionaries.

Why Not to Support National Missionaries

1. *Unilateral or one-sided financial support creates undue dependency*

When the donor partner (assumed to be the Western World partner) provides too much of the overall financing for the mission work, an unhealthy parent-child dynamic can set in. This is not a new criticism, as the study of John Nevius' writings would show. Along with Roland Allen and the aforementioned

Rufus Anderson and Henry Venn, John Nevius was in the
vanguard of the movement that called for the indigenisation of
foreign missionary work. This Presbyterian missionary to
Shangtung, China in the nineteenth century (1829–1893)
devised a strategy which promoted the concept of voluntary
(unpaid) evangelists.[5] These national workers were to be
tentmakers, that is, remaining in their own vocation so they
could support themselves without having to depend on the foreign missionary, while carrying on the work of the ministry.
Roland Allen perpetuated this philosophy that 'he who has the
gold, rules' in decrying early twentieth-century mission field
strategy, which still struggled with passing on the reins of
power from Western missionary to national church, without
allowing the newly established church to be unduly dependent
on her spiritual parents. Hear him critique the financial
dependence of national on foreigner in his ground-breaking,
Missionary Methods: St Paul's Or Ours?:

> The natives always speak of 'the Mission' as something
> which is not their own. The Mission represents a foreign
> power, and natives who work under it are servants of a
> foreign Government. It is an evangelistic society, and the
> natives tend to leave it to do the evangelistic work that
> properly belongs to them. It is a model, and the natives
> learn simply to imitate it. It is a wealthy body, and the
> natives tend to live upon it, and expect it to supply all
> their needs. Finally, it becomes a rival, and the native
> Christians feel its presence as an annoyance, and they
> envy its powers; it becomes an incubus, and they groan
> under the weight of its domination.[6]

This viewpoint has not died away, in spite of colonialism fad-
ing into the distance, and with it, the free access of missionaries
to many of their traditional mission fields. A survey of articles
in the last two decades of the missiological journal, *Evangelical*

---

[5] John Nevius, *Planting and Development of Missionary Churches* rev. ed.
(Phillipsburg, PA: Presbyterian and Reformed Publishing House, 1958).
[6] Roland Allen, *Missionary Methods: St. Paul's Or Ours?* (London: World
Dominion Press, 1930), p. 110.

Missions Quarterly, reveals that this issue continues to be a concern for practitioners of cross-cultural missions.[7] In summing up these money tensions, Don Hamilton says: 'In the past tensions have developed because of . . . the Western penchant of attaching strings to their gifts.'[8]

2. *Outside financial help corrupts the national missionary*

More harmful is the charge that Westerners spoil Two-Thirds World national workers when they uncritically send money because almost without exception the receiving countries are not as well off economically as the donor partner countries. Again the Three-Self Movement and their spokesmen like Nevius and Allen led the way in documenting how 'rice Christians' were the result, the legacy of Western missionaries' generosity and inability to contextualise their message and methods of cross-cultural communication of the Gospel. Today questions still exist over such things as the validity of statistics nationals publish about results from their ministries or the accuracy of prayer letters/reports in order to make sure that the money keeps coming from the West.[9]

The charge is increasingly being levelled that some national missionaries/church leaders and their agencies/ denominations are shaping their ministries so as to attract foreign money. Hence, for example, we hear Ott arguing that 'all too often native pastors and churches have become preoccupied with ministries that attract Western dollars (such as orphan work), while neglecting more basic pastoral care and evangelism.'[10] We see that this is not a new problem, for genera-

---

[7] See Vinay Samuel and C. Corwin, 'Assistance Programs Require Partnership,' *EMQ* 15(2) (April, 1979): 99; E. Madeira, 'Roots of Bad Feelings: What the Locals Say,' *EMQ* 19(2) (April, 1983): 104; C. Ott, 'Let the Buyer Beware,' *EMQ* 29(3) (July, 1993): 288; G. J. Schwartz, 'It's Time To Get Serious About the Cycle of Dependence in Africa,' *EMQ* 28(2) (April, 1993): 126–130.

[8] Don Hamilton, 'Report of the Ad Hoc Committee On Relations With Third World Missions.' In *Readings In Third World Missions: A Collection of Essential Documents*, ed. Marlin Nelson (Pasadena, CA: William Carey Library, 1978), p. 213.

[9] R. Stanley, 'The Curse of Money On Missions To India,' *EMQ* 21(3) (July, 1985): 294–297.

[10] Ott, *EMQ*. p. 289.

tions ago John Nevius, for one, stated that 'the Employment System [pay by foreign missionaries] tends to excite a mercenary spirit, and to increase the number of mercenary Christians. . . . When this mercenary spirit enters a church, it has a wonderful self-propagatory power and follows the universal law of propagating after its kind.'[11]

Sometimes the sharpest critics are national missions' leaders themselves. Listen to five Indians speak about their own people.[12]

- Vishal Mangalwadi, popular author of Christian books in India and the West: 'The Westerner must resist the temptation to start projects and employ new converts. So that all who come to Christ, and stay with him, do so exclusively because they are attracted by Christ Himself and not by money.'

- Kingley Kumar, leader with the Friends Missionary Prayer Band: 'Western agencies should not support individuals who do not have an accountable relationship with any association or umbrella organization in India. Therefore, a great amount of money is being given which is not being invested in missions. They merely use it in building up themselves and those around them. This is one of the sad state of affairs in India.'

- Atul Aghamkar, professor at Union Biblical Seminary in Pune: 'Sending just money is often risky, since you do not know how the money is being used. In some cases the money is not needed. In those instances the monetary gift serves only to place the recipient body in a chronically dependent state. Money for maintenance purposes should be eliminated. Periodic visits and evaluations of projects, ministries and programs should be made to ensure accountability.'

- Sam Kamaleson, Vice President of World Vision: 'Western money can rob the initiative of sacrificial giving from within India itself. It creates in the already

---

[11] Nevius, *Planting*, p. 15.
[12] Quoted in 'India's Mission Leaders Speak To the Western Church,' *Mission Frontier*. (November-December, 1994).

suspicious mindset of the non-Christian the idea that
Western Christian engagement in mission within India
is purely mercenary.'

- T. V. Thomas, president of the North American Council
For South Asian Christians: 'Constant supply of funds
from the West could create a weak Christian and a
weak church in India. This has been the pattern in many
areas in the past. I believe that indigenous funding
needs to increase as the church matures.'

3. *Support of nationals creates a credibility gap with the national church*

Related to the previous point is the fact that when Western-
based donor partners underwrite salaries of national
missionaries or church leaders, almost invariably such salaries
are higher than the nationals would have received from
locally-derived giving only. This can create a credibility gap
with the emerging church. Motives of the workers may be ques-
tioned. All the church goer back in the West sees is that so little
is being done for the national missionary's family because, after
all, 'we only give them $200.00 per month and those are starva-
tion wages'. But if the average church member of the national
church, which the national missionary is planting, is only earning $100.00 per month, then by comparison, the national
missionary is living off the fat of the land! It's all relative.

The fact of the matter is that in many undeveloped or semi-
developed countries $1 or £1 can buy an awful lot of bananas
or rice or millet! Therefore, throwing money at Two-Thirds
World mission agencies and new churches is not necessarily a
good thing. Roger Hedlund, long-time expatriate missionary
and missiologist in India alludes to the problem with this comment: 'Insensitive international Christian organisations . . .
pre-empt local initiative, siphon off choice leadership, and create an inflated parachurch economy. The foreign missionaries
of the past apparently were more sensitive to local conditions
and personnel needs than are a number of their bureaucratic
successors.'[13]

---

[13] Roger Hedlund, *Evangelisation and Church Growth: Issues From the Asian Context* (Madras: McGavran Institute, 1992), p. 123.

What's worse is that this discrepancy in wages can be a greater stumbling block and source of misunderstanding to the non-Christian. The average man on the street, observing the relative wealth of the foreign-paid missionary or pastor, may assume he has been paid off or has a calculating spirit in going about his employment. Thus, the stereotype of Christianity being a Western religion is perpetuated. This may be a greater problem in nations previously colonised by Western World powers. Then too, in Muslim cultures, the concept of a 'full-time' religious worker is foreign. Their mullahs (Muslim priests) generally have 'secular' jobs and do their 'pastoring' on a part-time basis. On the other hand, the Brahmin priests of Hinduism are used to having every need catered for by local or pilgriming Hindu devotees.

It is difficult to generalise, but perception can be a problem, whether within or outside the national church. As Samuel Escobar observes: 'Highly specialised parachurch organizations are causing havoc in Third World countries by the procedure of hiring top leaders at salary levels that distance them too much from their colleagues in national churches and denominational jobs. . . . Parachurch organizations need to be delivered from their Messianic complexes.'[14]

4. Obsession with support of nationals saps the church in the west of its sending vitality

One of the most telling criticisms is that once the Western World church stops sending its own flesh and blood into missions it will lose its vision for the larger unreached world. Wade Coggins, former director of the EFMA, one of the largest umbrella agencies for mission agencies in North America, rightly and early on in the debate, pinpointed such one-sided involvement in missions as being a dangerous precedent. In his article 'Can God No Longer Afford North American Missionaries?', published in the *Evangelical Missions Quarterly*, he argues that, 'If the American church begins to give only its money, and not its sons and daughters to missions, the

---

[14] Escobar, speech, 1991.

missionary vision will be dead in a generation or less.'[15]
Although leaders of organisations majoring on support of
nationals insist that they are not trying to paint an either/or
picture, you realise this is not the message that some of them
actually send, when you study their books or their promo-
tional mouthpieces. Witness, for instance, K. P. Yohannan in
full gear in his initial book on this subject: 'Until we can recog-
nize the native missionary movement as the plan of God for
this period of history, and until we are willing to become servants of what He is doing, we're in danger of frustrating the
will of God.'[16] Pioneer of the modern movement to support
nationals Allen Finley, tends to be even more rhetorical and
combatative in calling the Western World church to shift its
resources from Westerners to nationals.

However, there is no escaping the fact – whether or not it is
pragmatic for European and North American churches to
continue to send their own missionaries so as to keep the missions' vision alive – that the Bible says, 'Go', it does not just
say, 'Give'. The heart of the Great Commission is captured in
the *going*, whether you read it in Matthew, Luke, Mark, or
John! In God the Father sending His Son, we have the model of
how to do missions. This is an incarnational ministry, embodied in actually going physically cross-culturally to those in
need. Fulfilling the Great Commission cannot be reduced to
cost effectiveness.

In all fairness, leaders of the agencies specialising in support
of nationals are beginning to rectify the damage done by an
extreme form of promoting nationals. In an interview with me,
Grover Grosby, Canadian Director of Partners International,
pointedly claimed that he discouraged churches from shifting
all their mission dollars to support nationals. He felt that in the
long run it would undercut their commitment to missions in
general because failure to send their own would demotivate
churches from giving at all. He saw the old principle of 'out of
sight, out of mind' at work in a new way.

---

[15] *EMQ* 24(3) (July, 1988): 205.
[16] K. P. Yohannan, *Revolution in World Missions*, rev. ed. (Altamonte Springs,
FL: Creation House, 1992), p. 152.

National leaders themselves are wary of Western churches jumping off the bandwagon of supporting nationals. Chris Marantika, Indonesian founder of the Evangelical Theological Seminary in Indonesia, which has planted hundreds of churches through theological students, and popular spokesman for Partners International in the West, says this: 'It is unbiblical not to send missionaries. But it is also unbiblical not to support nationals, because we are one body. I do believe we have to work as partners.'[17]

In like vein, black South African missiologist Ebenezer Sikakane, recently retired professor of missions at Ontario Bible College in Toronto, observes:

> In the middle of these developments [rapid increase of national missionaries], Western missionaries cannot withdraw, thinking that their work is complete. The Great Commission has not been rescinded and Western missionaries still have a vital role to play. Sheer numbers dictate this. It would take a long time, for example, for Indian missionaries to evangelize India with a population soon to reach one billion and a present Christian population of under two per cent![18]

Finally, Joseph D'Souza, Executive Director of OM-India, argues: 'The idea that the West should only send money is neither biblically sound nor a very practical idea for India of the nineties. While it is true that the dollar can go a long way here, limiting partnership to the contribution of money is an inadequate opting out of cross-cultural mission. Western participation in Indian mission must be total, including prayer, personnel, finances, expertise, etc.'[19]

---

[17] Chris Marantika, 'An Indonesian Leader Speaks Out to the Church in the West,' *EMQ* 26(1) (January, 1990): 10.
[18] Ebenezer Sikakane, 'Two-Thirds World Missionaries Need Western Partners,' *Christian Week* (April 13, 1993).
[19] Quoted in *Mission Frontiers*, p. 3.

5. Dependence on foreign money will undermine the commitment of local christians to tithe

This is a very real fear that has been reinforced by the dubious track record of some national churches in the Two-Thirds World. There are some shining exceptions to the rule of poor-, giving churches in the newly-developing world, such as the church in Burma and the church in Korea. Many national Christians have given in the same way as Paul described the giving of the Macedonian churches: 'Out of the most severe trial, their overflowing joy and their extreme poverty welled up in rich generosity' (2 Cor. 8:2). Let's face the facts. The prosperity and dominance of Western missionaries in many Two-Thirds World settings have desensitised national Christians to biblical forms of financial stewardship.

It's not a new problem, but one that has been around since the early days of the modern missionary movement. Witness what John Nevius said 150 years ago in decrying the tendency of missionaries to hire national evangelists: 'The Apostle in the ninth chapter of First Corinthians lays down the general rule that, as a matter of right, the teacher should depend for his temporal support on the taught; still in first introducing the Gospel to a heathen people, he felt it his duty to waive this privilege. . . . I believe it is best, at least in the first stage of mission work, for the native missionary to follow Paul's example.'[20] Voicing a similar concern in the early 1900s is Roland Allen: 'That one Church should depend upon another [the churches of the Western missionary] for the supply of its ordinary expenses as a Church, or even for a part of them, would have seemed incredible in the Four Provinces. From this apostolic practice we are now as far removed in action as we are in time.'[21]

6. Tensions arise in the relationship when money is at the heart of it

Some argue, probably from experience, that unnecessary tensions occur between emerging and sending church when

---

[20] Nevius, *Planting*, p. 22.
[21] Allen, *Missionary Methods*, p. 70.

outside financial support of the local work takes place. Suspicions arise at either end of the relationship. Sending partners worry that money may be misappropriated because they are not close at hand to verify proper use of funds.

Temptation to exaggerate results to please donors is a very real one and is a major cause of suspicion in donor countries. In 1997 while visiting national church planters in Rajasthan in India, I showed one of them the report of a Western-based fund-raising agency claiming that in 1996 their workers in India had baptised 2500 people. I was assured that their work in Rajasthan, among the tribals especially, was highly exaggerated.

On the other hand, nationals often get resentful or annoyed when they see captions under photos of themselves, often used without permission, that pass off the national missionary as 'our' (read Western-owned) church planter or evangelist. Sometimes the national may receive support from three different sources in the West, each source claiming the results as his or her own! Commenting on this sort of problem, Madeira says: 'Nationals resent the fact that missionaries often use them for fund-raising purposes, by claiming support is needed for Christian workers (taking their pictures), scholarships for students, money for building projects, bringing in money to the coffers of the society that never benefits the persons, places or projects represented. They feel like they are being exploited for personal financial gain.'[22]

7. Outside financial help obscures proper financial accountability

A final criticism of receiving financial help from abroad is that it prevents a reasonable degree of financial accountability over monies given to the local ministry. Araujo defines *accountability* in a missions' sense as 'a willingness to place oneself under someone else's review and examination concerning one's motives, actions, and outcomes according to mutually agreed upon expectations, in an environment of good faith and mutual

---

[22] Madeira, EMQ: 102.

trust.'[23] Certainly, national churches or missions that accept money gladly, without offering any verification that the money is being used for the purpose given, are equally as guilty of poor accountability as the donor is in not insisting that some sort of accounting mechanism be put in place.

Most groups specialising in support of nationals go to great lengths to establish reporting-back procedures. For instance, Partners International will only work through existing national agencies which have their own boards and will not otherwise support nationals directly. However, it must be noted that government-imposed standards for non-profit (not-for-profit) agencies or charities in some Two-Thirds World countries do not approach the strict standards of those in many Western countries. It is not unusual for some of these national ministries to fill their boards with relatives of the founder or director. The idea of potential conflict of interest is a missing concept in the minds of such national leaders. Also missing in numerous cases, is the concept of an outside, that is, an independent, audit. Annually audited statements, whether done by an internal or external (the latter kind being the preferred form) auditor, are too often considered an anathema. Perhaps a lonely church planter among Muslims in Kazakhstan does not need an external audit, but some of these national ministries are not small. Hundreds of national missionaries may be employed and co-ordinated through a sizeable administrative office without even an internal audit being done regularly.

As one talks to agencies in the West who promote support of nationals, one gets the sense that the real accountability going on is limited at best. Partners International say that periodically their leaders and church leaders involved with them from the West visit the front lines to see for themselves the alleged ministries that are going on. Well and good. But usually having announced months in advance that they are coming! Who wouldn't put on their best front under such circumstances?

[23] A. Araujo, 'Confidence Factors: Accountability in Christian Partnerships.' in *ingdom Partnership For Synergy in Missions*, ed. William Taylor (Pasadena, CA: illiam Carey Library, 1994), p. 121.

Add to that the visitors' unfamiliarity with the local culture, the vast time zone changes faced by them on a whirlwind trip, and the likely grappling to one degree or another with Montezuma's Revenge (diarrhoea or some other similar reaction to the local food and water!), and you are faced with the likelihood that the foreigner will be too distracted to discern what is really happening in the indigenous ministry he or she is seeing, perhaps for the first time.

Gospel For Asia, cognisant of this problem, has established the practice of making these survey trips unannounced. While this may obviate the dilemma of proper accountability somewhat, the fact is that such secretive trips are done by the national GFA leaders, not the visitors from the West. In other words, it is not the people giving the money, but the people receiving the money who are evaluating the validity of ministry which, incidentally, affects their means of livelihood too. Aware of this conflict of interest, in recent years, Revenue Canada, the arm of federal government policing registered charities in Canada, such as churches, has ruled that pastors or any employees of a charity who receive remuneration from that charity, cannot vote in any board meeting of the charity. They can only serve as ex-officio members of the board only. This is a shrewd and wise decision, in my opinion. It deals with the very sort of problem we are talking about here with regard to national ministries supported from offshore.

Interestingly enough, Canada is an international leader in this whole field of calling registered charities to account. Governments in the West are preoccupied with this field because they lose tax revenues by granting tax-exempt status to charities and/or tax deductible privileges to the charities whereby donors to those charities are able to reduce their taxes paid according to the level of donations given to the registered charities. Revenue Canada has tightened up standards for Canadian charities sending money offshore. Such charities now must establish joint venture agreements with the organisations or charities in the countries with which they want to do business, in such a way that the use of the money is closely monitored so as to ensure Canadian control over the joint ministry proportionate to the share of the resourcing of the joi-

ministry. While this measure may seem overbearing, or appear to be a form of reverting to colonial rule, you can't help feeling empathy with governments who are frustrated by fraudulent use of charitable monies, such as evidenced in the Jimmy Bakker scandal of a few years ago. In their way of thinking, a concession has been made (surrender of tax revenues by the government) which has been abused. While British, American, and German governments have slightly different agendas from Canada's in regulating registered charities that have global reaches, it is only likely that their governments' controls will tighten in the name of accountability.

However, those affected the most by this way of thinking about accountability, the nationals themselves, do not always see things the same way. They accuse Westerners of stirring up a tempest in a tea pot! A survey I did of thirty top OM Indian leaders in 1993 unearthed some fascinating results: 57 per cent of the respondents felt that at least half of OM-India's money should be derived from within India itself in order for OM-India to be considered 'indigenised'.[24] However, only approximately 10 per cent of OM-India monies actually originates in India. But 82 per cent of these same respondents felt the Indian church viewed OM-India as 'quite indigenised' or 'moderately indigenised'.[25] They felt that was an accurate view of the nature of things.

In answer to the question in the survey which asked respondents to rank what types of issues were important for Indian OMers, in order for them to sense that there was an equal partnership between themselves and the rest of the OM world, financial self-support was ranked as being the least important, garnering only 12 per cent of the weighted share of votes.

Such ambivalence about the importance of the financial issue is consistent with their leader's statements made during

---

[4] 'Indigenised' is considered to be different from 'indigenous'. 'Indigenous' ~~fe~~rs to ministry begun locally and which continues to be supported locally. ~~In~~digenised' implies that the ministry began with ex-patriate influence or ~~n~~ative, but has now been taken over by the locals (nationals).

~~O~~M-India was begun by ex-patriates in 1963 and so cannot be considered ~~ind~~igenous'. The work didn't begin in India. However it can be viewed as ~~indig~~nised'.

an interview I did with him in January, 1993 in Hyderabad. At that time, Joseph D'Souza saw no discrepancy between the fact that less than a quarter of OM-India's funding was derived from within India and his understanding that OM-India was relatively indigenised. He said: 'The Indian Mission Association, which used to have a policy that 100 per cent of the funds for a mission had to come from within India, has now done a complete about-face. . . . OM is now a full-fledged indigenised mission by their present definition.'[26]

To be fair, Joseph is concerned to see more and more revenues for OM-India generated from within India. In this regard he has gone on record as saying that 'as long as the Indian church generously and consistently supports the work of OM, the amount of money coming from abroad is not a significant issue.' In a similar vein, a former senior OM-India leader, Divakaran, maintains that 'as long as the amount of money from within India grows substantially each year, the amount of money coming from abroad is not an issue.'

Positive Reasons for Support of Nationals

1. *The self-support philosophy breeds selfishness because it focuses on 'self'*

There have probably been fewer vociferous critics of the Three-Self Movement than that great Indian Christian, now deceased, Bishop V. S. Azariah. In his monograph, *Christian Giving*, he says that 'the goal of self-support can become a real hindrance to the full development of the churches [of India] . . . [resulting in] paying little attention to evangelism.'[27] The suggestion is that the striving for independence encapsulated in the three 'selfs' is more characteristic of the independence and individualism endemic in the West than it is of a biblical view

---

[26] The India Mission Association is an umbrella agency of national parachurch ministries similar to the WEF or the IFMA. Joseph's comment on the IMA change in definition was verified by a subsequent interview I had with IMA Executive Director, Ebenezer Sunder Raj, on January 31, 1993.
[27] V. S. Azariah, *Christian Giving* (New York: Associated Press, 1955), p.

of things. Instead of the focus being Christward and outward, it is reflective of a self-absorbed nationalism. Thus we find critics of the Three-Self Movement like Warren Webster saying, 'A church which is too *self*-conscious may be also *self*-centred and *self*fish, and not infrequently this has been a failing of so-called "indigenous" churches established as a result of this ideology.'[28] The long and short of it is: Can we say that it ought to be the goal of any church to be self-sufficient and independent from any other part of the Body of Christ? Are we not brothers and sisters of one another in a universal Family?

2. *Self-support shifts attention away from the important goal of being self-propagating*

If the goal being promoted is independence from the 'mother' church(es), it is far easier to measure such separation through financial criteria and leadership criteria than anything else. Hence the national church or agency leadership tends to focus on the immediate and tangible, neglecting proactive aspects of ministry like winning souls to Christ or planting new churches. Evangelism suffers as 'pastors have become little more than money-making machines'.[29]

Missionary statesman, Herbert Kane, rightly grasped this dilemma in his astute statement:

> By and large it is true to say that we [missionaries from the West] did not plant *missionary* churches. The churches were supposed to be self-governing, self-supporting, and self-propagating. The churches emphasized the first, self-government. The missions attached great importance to the second, self-support. Neither church nor mission attached equal importance to the third, self-propagation.[30]

---

[28] Warren Webster, 'Aiding Emerging Churches Overseas in Developing a Missions Strategy.' in *Readings in Third World Missions: A Collection of Essential Documents*, ed. Marlin L. Nelson (Pasadena, CA: William Carey Library, 1978), 38. For similar sentiments see Peter Beyerhaus, 'The Three-Selves Formula – Built On Biblical Foundations?' *International Review of Missions* 10: 393–407. zariah, *Christian Giving*, p. 43.

rbert Kane, 'Evangelization: Problem of National Missions.' in Nelson,

Perhaps this is an oversimplification of what went on, but the point is well made. In hindsight, most mission strategists would like to see aspects of all three in place.

3. *Obsession with the financial side of the partnership overshadows other contributions the younger partner can make in the relationship*

It is all too easy to assume that the relationship is one-way – from the donor partner to the receiving partner in the Two-Thirds World. The Bible expositor at the 1996 annual autumn international conference of OM, which was held at De Bron, Holland was Joseph D'Souza. In front of almost one thousand night people night after night he ministered the Word of God in a very capable way, drawing on experiences from his unique vantage point in Asia and from his agile, well-read mind to shed fresh light on Scriptural truths. Church leaders from the Two-Thirds World are desperately needed as voices in the West to fan the flame, to revitalise flagging zeal and failing faith.

It is my own impression that one of the greatest contributions the recipient partner (of finances) can make to the partnership is prayer. Many Latin, African, and Asian Christians are great prayer warriors. My wife has suffered two ongoing heart problems, hepatitis and subsequent liver problems, rheumatic fever, six lots of major surgery to deal with growths, including a cancerous one on her bladder, and a non-functioning thyroid. Although obviously I cannot prove it, it is my deeply settled conviction that she is alive today because of the faithful prayers over many years by numerous Indian Christians (and others of course). Whenever I go to India I am besieged by Indian friends wanting information about how Linda is doing. Quite often the quizzing is ended by the comment that they pray for her health every day! What a tremendous contribution the Indian church can make to the church in Great Britain, her former coloniser, for instance, by interceding as one standing in the gap for her in th face of spiritual decline.

Reflecting on this aspect of partnership whereby attentio given to more than just money, Samuel Escobar says:

The internationalization of mission will require a disposition to accept partnerships in which leaders come from a variety of backgrounds and experiences. The partners in these new schemes will be contributing to mission in different ways. One of the most important principles of interaction will be that those who contribute financially the most may not happen to be the ones that will provide the leadership in terms of spiritual maturity, theology, methods, and strategies. I have found this to be the most difficult principle to accept for North Americans. Partly because in missionary practice usually money has had strings attached, and partly because here we are dealing with a deeply ingrained characteristic of their national ethos at this point in history. I believe that true fellowship, friendship, and trust are the kind of spiritual infrastructure that makes international partnerships possible.[31]

Younger churches in the East *do* want to make a return to the older churches of the West which have spawned them, whether by ministering through spiritual gifts, or whatever. Let us not deny them the experience of it being more blessed to give than to receive.

4. Classical missionary work involves evangelism and planting the church, which, by definition, means that outside support is essential

Nascent churches being established where there is no church, such as in the mountains of Uzbekistan, or in the deserts of Mauritania, will not be in a position to support their own pastor for some years. Those involved are the pioneer missionaries in particular who need support from the outside. Once a church is well-rooted, we can understand why it might be expected that the new church be relatively or completely self-sufficient financially. Too often the issue is confused in the sense that no distinction is made in strategic thinking between the fledgling church being planted and the mature church now established.

Escobar, speech, 1991.

Missionary thinking and maintenance thinking are two different animals requiring two different feeding programmes. So
says Harvey Conn in his thought-provoking article, 'The
Money Barrier Between Sending and Receiving Churches':

> It is my contention that behind this formulation
> ['self-support'] is the hidden curriculum that assumes a
> double standard for funding, built on an invisible distinc-
> tion between 'sending church' and 'receiving' church. . . .
> Is not the Pauline pattern (1 Cor. 9:14) one of support for
> the ministry (whether expatriate or national) from the
> church in which he labors? What's wrong with foreign
> (receiving church) money for foreign (sending church)
> missionaries? Can we recover the Pauline concept of eco-
> nomic participation in the ministry as 'fellowship in the
> Gospel' (Phil. 1:5) by asking *only* for 'foreign money
> for national pastors' and not also for 'national money for
> foreign pastors'?[32]

In other words, let us be careful that we have not built into the
nature of things in missions, a preconceived notion that young
Christians or new churches do not inherently have the ability
to make sacrifices or reciprocate blessing. Partnership is a
two-way street and the sooner we give the opportunity for
'receiving churches', or agencies, to demonstrate their spiritual
riches, the stronger and more genuine the partnership will be.
One way that will be displayed is through receiving partners
learning to give financially. And sending partners learning to
receive financially!

Again, a distinction needs to be made between fledgling
churches and more established, planted churches. One rule of
thumb we could adopt is that churches which are five years old
or more should have reached the point in their size and
discipling where they no longer need to be recipients of outside
funding.[33] The church-planting missionary who now stays on
would then be viewed as a pastor, not a missionary! Just as if he
or she passes over the reins of leadership to a national, that

[32] EMQ 14(4) (Oct., 1978): 233, 235.
[33] Beyerhaus, *Int. Review*, 1964: 401–402.

national would be perceived as a pastor and not as a missionary. We are reminded of what Galatians 6 teaches in this regard: 'Anyone who receives instruction in the Word must share all good things with his instructor' (See also, 1 Cor. 9:14, 18). National churches should not adopt a totally self-sufficient mentality, nor should they adopt a total dependence mentality. Each church should learn to carry its own burden (Gal. 6:5), but at the same time other churches should be prepared to carry the burdens of the less fortunate (Gal. 6:2).

5. Providing financial support for nationals enables donor partners to develop servanthood

There is great joy in tithing and in giving special offerings to the Lord's work. Apart from leading individuals to the saving knowledge of Christ, I know, personally speaking, of no greater joy in Christian living. In serving others, practically and materially, we walk in the Christ-like way of servanthood. The history of missions has shown that simply delivering the almighty dollar or pound to the front lines has not proved that donors have humble, servant hearts. There have often been heavy-handedness and lengthy strings attached to donations, some of which have not always been compatible with the goal of establishing the church cross-culturally. But certainly if there is no right opportunity provided for giving, provision for demonstrating servanthood has been hamstrung.[34] Especially if decision making is primarily left in the hands of the nationals doing the bulk or all of the actual on-site ministry, servanthood is being expressed by the donor partner.[35] As Western World Christians enter global partnerships for penetrating the final frontiers with the Gospel, we need to relinquish traditional Two-Thirds World power bases while continuing to supply financial support judiciously. Then indigenisation occurs naturally, not forced through a formula, but nevertheless in a way

Samuel and Corwin, EMQ: 98.

For an insight into more of the dynamics often associated with giving by donors to poorer partners in global arrangements see Ajith Fernando, " and "Poor" Nations and the Christian Enterprise: Some Personal nts,' *Missiology: An International Review* 9(3) (July, 1981): 287–298.

that allows the Gospel to be authenticated locally (contextual-ised), balanced with co-operation from the larger Body of Christ, of which each local expression is a part.

6. Too much emphasis on self-support can be a form of reverse paternalism

I have observed this kind of paternalism first-hand through my years of service with OM-India. Early on in OM-India's history, in the sixties and seventies, there appeared to be an unfortunate judging of Indian motives concerning financial matters. It was considered undesirable for Indian OMers to go abroad, for example. Direct contact with foreign donors was frowned upon. Excerpts from an open letter circulated in my first years in India in the early seventies, 'Important Memo To All Indian OMers' substantiate my assertion. This leadership letter stated the following:

> There is a real danger that people [Indians] will join OM or the [OM] ship as a stepping stone to 'get ahead in the world'.... Soon they will be off to [other] lands to 'minister' but in fact their motives are mixed.... We must face the fact that most people are desperate to get ahead in life, to be somebody, and to get material things and this desperateness will lead them into subtle forms of self-deception.

WOW!! By *reverse paternalism* we mean that assumptions are made about the Two-Thirds World church that characterise it as less spiritually mature than the Western World church. By insisting that these nationals stand on their own two feet finan-cially without any outside help is just a subtle way of saying that they are different from us, that we don't want to spoil them. Setting up higher or lower standards for them than we do for ourselves is just a form of reverse paternalism. Self-criticism of the Western World missionary enterprise rarely occur Gnats are strained over Two-Thirds World unspirituality wh camels are swallowed about Western World faults.

A case in point concerns missionary finances. Jon Bon argued convincingly in his prophetic treatise, *Mone*

Missions, that Western World missionaries have lived too lavishly on the mission field – maybe not by their homeland standards, but almost inevitably by the standards of the people they are trying to reach. In many cases, their lifestyles have alienated them from the very people for whom they have made 'sacrifices'. The indictment of missionary lifestyles (lifestyles complete with imported washers and dryers, sometimes even cars!) by proponents of support-of-nationals is therefore understandable.[36] At the risk of over-generalising, this problem of a too-high lifestyle seems to be more of a problem for missionaries of denominational as opposed to interdenominational (or non-denominational) mission boards/agencies, and of North American more than European missionaries.

Probably the main reason why OM caused a shock effect to ripple through the missionary community when it first went to India in 1963 was that the white-skinned foreigners lived the same way as their Indian co-workers. They did not live in missionary compounds, complete with a Westernised subculture; but ate in the same dirty, road-side hotels, travelled in the same third-class, unreserved train compartments, slept on the same sleeping blankets on the floor, and took their baths in the same buckets of unheated water, one bucket to soap down, and another to rinse off. Those were heady days. We can do it, we said! What a statement of the oneness of the Body of Christ this made to the Indian church, even though some of us did get sick with hepatitis, some were self-righteous about our simple living, and some did not last more than that initial two year short term missions' stint!

Back to the point. Western World Christians have no monopoly on spirituality and so we have to be careful we do not treat Two-Thirds World Christians as second-class citizens in the Kingdom of God, who somehow need to be re-colonised again, even if a little more humanely this time round! If the truth were known, we have a lot to be humble about and a lot to learn from our brethren in far-flung corners of the globe.

An example of this indictment is in K. P. Yohannan, *Why the World Waits: ɔsing the Reality of Modern Missions* rev. ed. (Lake Mary, FL.: Creation House,), p. 161.

7. Too much concentration on 'indigeneity' hinders the development of 'missionary' churches

The Three-Self Movement, as we have seen, with its drive to produce indigenised churches, tended to breed a superficial focus on only two of the selves: self-support and self-government. Self-propagation went the way of all flesh. William Smalley addressed this problem when he said:

> It may be very easy to have a self-governing church which is not indigenous. . . . All that it is necessary to do is to indoctrinate a few leaders in Western patterns of church government, and let them take over. . . . It is the way funds are administered, the way decisions are made, and the purposes to which they are put that are diagnostic of an indigenous church, not the presence or absence of such foreign funds. . . Of the three 'selfs', it seems to me that self-propagating is the one most nearly diagnostic of an indigenous church.[37]

The appropriate goal of missions is as much to plant missionary churches as it is to plant indigenous churches.[38] Indeed, as we saw in chapter one, that is exactly what is happening now. The Two-Thirds World church has escaped the shackles of a misshapen theology (that had her too inward-looking) and has rediscovered the Great Commission. The balance must be maintained between believing God for an indigenous church and a missionary church. A later chapter will delve into that subject in more depth.

8. The undue emphasis on self-support obscures the needs of the unreached world

If over two billion people in the world can yet be classified as *unreached*, as authorities like Ralph Winter, David Barrett, and Patrick Johnstone insist, then a massive infusion of money and manpower needs to be injected into the bloodstream of

---

[37] William Smalley, 'Cultural Implications of an Indigenous Church.' in *Readings In Dynamic Indigeneity*, eds. Charles H. Kraft and Tom N. Wisley (Pasadena, CA: William Carey Library, 1979), pp. 32, 34, 35.

[38] Webster, *Readings* p. 38.

existing efforts to fulfil the Great Commission. And given the fact that the most intractable, unevangelised areas are primarily in countries not allowing missionary visas – like most of the 44 countries with a Muslim majority – so that only tentmakers can advance the Gospel, the call for labourers for the harvest fields remains strong. Where 'missionaries' can only witness in their spare time in order to retain residency in the country, the amount of time given to evangelism or pastoral work will be limited. Thus Ted Yamamori in *God's New Envoys* advances the argument that two hundred thousand new tentmakers are needed to bring closure to world evangelisation.

What am I trying to say? Just this. We need each other in the battle. Two-Thirds World missionaries are not a panacea for world evangelisation. Neither are Western World missionaries. All types of Spirit-filled missionaries are needed, from whatever part of the world they might come. So, if the release of Two-Thirds World missionaries is partially dependent on Western World capitalisation, then let's not quibble too much over whether that undermines indigeneity.

Having made a case for both supporting and not supporting nationals, the reader is left to weigh the evidence. My conviction is that we should err on the side of supporting nationals if we are not clear which way to go. Nevertheless, we should do so while not neglecting to support our own; those going out from our own church and nation for whom we have a unique stewardship. Furthermore, we should screen nationals carefully, scrutinising the plethora of opportunities presenting themselves to us from the Two-Thirds World and from the Western-based organisations that often front for them. Come what may, we need to face up to the fact that it is unlikely that we can finish the job of world evangelisation without a growing network of global partnerships emerging.

SIX

The Fascinating Tale of OM-India

Should we take the national missionary movement seriously? One of the ways to answer that question is to take an inside look at what God is doing through specific national mission organisations in the Two-Thirds World. That is what we attempt to do in this chapter by briefly telling the story of Operation Mobilisation in India, a ministry which began thirty years ago and today features seven hundred national missionaries.

It all began when a bedraggled, sorry-looking band of foreigners limped into New Delhi on a cool morning back in November, 1963. They had driven overland from Brussels on the so-called Asian highway for about 10,000 kilometres, with the intention of sharing their faith with the people of India. Speaking of that eventful trip, Greg Livingstone, who was eventually to become the founder and international director of Frontiers, had these things to say:

> When I told George Verwer I didn't even know where India was, he said, 'Go East – you can't miss it!' It took us two months to get there due to breaking an axle in the desert of Iran, and John Crisp (UK) getting deathly sick. This forced the group to turn back twice to Teheran as it approached the Afghanistan border. When we got to the Indian border, outside Lahore, we were told we had the wrong car papers and that they would not let th Volkswagen van into India. It has been sitting in Pakist rusting ever since! God used our simple faith as prayed that he would bring Indians into the work, look at what it is today!

They were mostly Britons and Americans, determined to work alongside their Indian brothers and sisters to proclaim the Gospel of Christ in the unevangelised North. Reared in an organisational setting, where material goods were shared in common and where a team approach to doing ministry was emphasised, these OMers didn't think twice about inviting Indian Christians to not only do evangelism with them, as the missionaries were prone to do, but to live with them 'on the road', going village to village, bazaar to bazaar, literally preaching the Gospel through translation in the open air. Others from the West soon joined them.

Often late in the evening, they would park their British lorries under the stars and spread their bedsheets on the roofs of the vehicles, sometimes waking up the next morning to a crowd of curious on-lookers. Since when did the white man sleep in anything other than a mansion? And shoulder to shoulder with Indians? The simple lifestyle of these foreigners and their willingness to treat their Indian counterparts as equals gradually attracted more and more Indian young people wanting to get training in basic discipleship and evangelism. They were drawn too by the rigorous way of life, beginning with callisthenics early in the morning and ending with an extended time of corporate prayer in the evenings.

Ministry centred in the states of Rajasthan, Bihar, and Karnataka. Even from the beginning the work was led by an Indian, Thomas Samuel, the man who had first invited OM to India. Before too long, the ministry had grown to two hundred people. In the first years, there seemed to be more Westerners than Indians on the teams, but gradually the tide began to turn. Teams were soon led by Indians, such as David Burder, and K. P. Yohannan; K. P. eventually left OM and started Gospel For Asia, a well-known ministry to nationals, headquartered in the United States.

Initially emphasis was on mass evangelism through literature distribution and open-air preaching. No churches were planted. Teams, made up mostly of novices, did their evangelism through local churches. Prospective OMers joined at the recommendation of their home church and after they had attended a training conference. Most stayed only for a two-year programme, but a number felt called to continue on long-term. In the early years, staying on was not a problem, at least for Commonwealth citizens, who were not required to get any sort of a visa for living in India.

Gradually the work expanded to other unreached states in the North, like West Bengal, Gujarat, and Uttar Pradesh. It wasn't too long before the organisers also discovered that with most of the Christians living in the extreme south of the country, they needed recruiting bases in states such as Kerala and Tamil Nadu. These were soon also opened up in cities like Bangalore, Madras, New Delhi, Ahmedabad, Ranchi, Ajmer, and Calcutta to service the teams in regional areas.

In 1973, a new era began as Ray Eicher and Alfy Franks took over as co-leaders of OM's work in India. Later that year, the first large-scale campaign united disparate parts of OM-India for a massive outreach in Bihar. Then in 1974 the first all-India outreach took place, called Reach-UP '74. For three months the teams closed down in all other areas of India and sowed the seed of the Gospel in every district of India's most populous state, Uttar Pradesh, where one hundred million people lived, and through which the Ganges River wound.

Organised by Chris Begg and myself, this programme solidified the vision of OM-India as never before. In some senses, this programme marked the coming of age of OM-India. Thirteen hundred people made professions of faith in an essentially Hindu part of the country and many of the Indian participants, in the excitement of seeing what God was doing through his 250 servants, decided then and there to give their lives to reaching the North and began believing in themselves. A year later, a second large-scale programme called Follow-UP '75, began to crystallise the leaders' thinking about the need to do more effective follow-up of response.

One of the young men who got his first introduction to OM-India life in Reach-UP '74 was Joseph D'Souza, from Belgaum in Karnataka, who had only recently graduated from university. I remember walking the streets of Agra, the home of the Taj Mahal, with Joseph in the evenings and having our hearts linked together in a deep way through our common burden for what we saw around us of the lostness of th

Hindu and Muslim masses. We dreamed of OM eventually nurturing communities of Christ followers (in a massive region of India) where believers literally averaged one in twenty thousand people. Leading one of the handful of church-based teams in 1975 that followed up on the most responsive areas in UP, Joseph began to develop his vision and theology of church-based evangelism and discipling which became a fundamental pillar of his philosophy of ministry later on when he took over leadership of OM-India.

In the meantime, OM-India continued to mature. A well-rounded training programme, developed under Joseph and Rajendran's leadership, began to provide team members, most of whom had never even been to Bible School, with the equivalent of a formal biblical education while allowing for focus to remain on field work and practical ministry. Learning by doing was still the emphasis, but that was balanced by regular doses of classroom teaching and team-based personal study.

The church grew in China after the missionaries left. A similar situation developed in India. Due to a further tightening of the visa situation in the country in the 1980s, gradually all the long-term foreigners had to leave. One or two, like Phillip Morris of England, continued to find ingenious ways to come and go, but, irreversibly, the reins of leadership had passed into the hands of the nationals. In spite of these changes (or because of them!) the work continued to prosper and grow. Giving increased from within India. A self-confidence and more contextualised way of operating emerged.

In 1989, Ray and Alfy resigned after years of exemplary servanthood leadership and Joseph D'Souza took up the reins of power. Now there were 350 people in OM. Many OM graduates had gone on into other parachurch ministries, started their own, or become pastors in local churches. A core of about thirty nationals provided stable and respected long-term leadership. They were the trainers of the trainees, the gurus of the shishyas (disciple in Hindi).

An example of one of these quality nationals the Lord gave OM as leaders was S. N. Shankar. Describing his testimony Shankar reminisces:

When I studied English literature at university, my Hindu professor told us to read the Bible. A Hindu friend who ran a second-hand bookstore gave me an old Bible. I read a few chapters, but did not read more.

Several months later I came to know an engineering student. Born a Hindu, he had become a follower of Christ. He explained that God is absolutely holy, and showed me that this same holy God is revealed in the person of Jesus Christ, and was interested in me as an individual. He went on to explain that Jesus had been killed and had risen from the dead.

He prayed a simple prayer asking Jesus to come in and change my life, which I repeated sentence by sentence. I did not feel radically different but I knew I was different. When I had finished my BA course, I wanted to share my faith with others, so I joined an OM team in my home state. Later two of my brothers decided to follow Christ.

Shankar now leads OM in all of South India and is one of the four main leaders of the entire work.

In the first few years under Joseph's leadership, OM-India moved into training and fielding friendship-evangelism teams working among Muslims and others working among Hindus. Since then OM has increasingly realised its responsibility to alleviate some of the awesome physical suffering still endemic to India. Thus, in the past few years, six teams have commenced holistic work among the poor in some of India's largest urban slums.

Most OMers, though, continue to see OM as a short-term training programme for themselves. Many Indian young people gain confidence in sharing their faith and cut their eye-teeth in ministry through a two or three year programme which has recently been given the right to grant a Bachelor of Ministry degree by an Indian evangelical accrediting body. Supplementing this, since 1995, has been a joint ventur Master of Arts in Leadership and Management or Missiolo degree programme between Briercrest Biblical Seminary Canada and OM-India. This non-residential, continu education programme is held on campus at the Hyde training centre twice a year for two weeks at a time. Currently there are thirty-five senior nationals enrolled in this programme with the first eight graduates expected in 1999. OM has trained ten thousand Indians in such ways over the last three decades.

Juxtapose those humble beginnings against the scene on January 1, 1997. PROJECT LIGHT was just a few months old. By the end of AD 2000, it was planned by the Indian leadership of OM, that their evangelism teams would meaningfully 'reach' multitudes of their own countrymen with the light of the Gospel. The OM teams got the Word out through evangelistic literature in the vernacular, the spoken word one-on-one, dramas such as those in the indigenous art form of bhajans, film ministry, and Gospel recordings for the illiterate.

Since PROJECT LIGHT began, the Holy Spirit's activity continues to be evident through Indian national missionaries on the OM teams. For instance, in a small town north of Calcutta life has remained the same for generations. The farmers rise very early and trudge to their farm lands humming their favourite Bengali cinema tunes as they prepare for a back-breaking day's work in the fields. But recently, one morning was different. Instead of going to the fields, thirteen adults gathered near a pond with Anil and Harish, OM workers. The cool breeze and the chirping birds filled the tranquil morning air. The villagers were gathering there for a special ceremony.

Anil waded slowly out into the water. Harish brought the onlookers one by one to Anil. There they received 'Jal Dikhya', in the name of the Father, the Son, and the Holy Spirit. Rising from the water radiant with joy, these Hindus had declared their allegiance to a new guru: the Lord Jesus Christ.

After months of teaching, shortly thereafter, Anil and Harish led a second group of new believers to the water's edge. After another open-air service, there was a communion time and a ve feast which lasted for hours, people were enjoying the owship so much. God was at work!

another part of North India, a different sort of ministry is ring through the teams involved in PROJECT LIGHT. ounds were hunters living in the forests of Ujain,

Madhya Pradesh (MP).[1] MP is the state of India, almost in its
centre, where the Hindi used is considered the purest spoken.
Gradually over the last four decades, the Gounds have moved
to Bhopal, the capital of MP, in search of a new life. Most have
wandered aimlessly, not finding adequate work and often on
the verge of starvation. Their main livelihood has been the
cruel job of breaking rock into gravel for construction companies. They do this by using small hammers to break the rocks
manually into fine stone.

To forget their torturous way of life, the Gounds have taken
to whiling away their evenings drinking alcohol. Even girls as
young as eight drink. What would you be tempted to do if you
were only earning 20 rupees a day (the equivalent of less than a
dollar or 50p) and then half the time you were being cheated
out of wages by exploitive contractors?!

Slowly building friendships with the Gounds, the OM team
responded to the Gounds' request to start a literacy
programme with them. Since April, 1996 literacy primers have
been used with the adults to teach them how to read and write
as well as how to understand the truths of the Bible, since the
primers are based on God's Word. Thus, the Gounds will
eventually have the opportunity to break their oppressive
cycle of poverty and to respond to the liberating power of the
Gospel.

Similar compassion-oriented ministries have begun in the
inner cities of Kanpur, Mumbai, Calcutta, Pune, Hyderabad,
and Bangalore over the last several years. They are called
GOOD SHEPHERD PROJECTS. Programmes range from
medical clinics to developing small business skills for single
mothers who have been deserted by abusive or substance-
abuse enslaved spouses. As a result of showing the love of
Christ practically, response has been amazingly quick in some
slums, slower in others. Good Shepherd teams in both
Hyderabad and Bombay have now seen communities of Chris

---

[1] This story is taken from a report by Debbie Meroff of OM's Interna
Coordinating Team based in Forest Hill, England.

followers established amongst the poorest of the poor. All this is being accomplished through nationals.

One such national on a Good Shepherd team is Annamma.[2] She joined OM in 1989, working on different types of evangelism teams. During this formative time, Annamma became exercised in spirit about the physical suffering of some of the poor she was stumbling across in the course of her outreach. At about the same time, the Lord was laying it on the hearts of OM leaders to start some sort of mercy ministry to the poor in one or two of India's mega-cities.

In 1992 after much prayer and discussion, a team of five young women was allowed to venture into the slum area of Hyderabad, called Rasulpur to start some sort of social programme among the poor. In 1992, Rasulpur was made up of five thousand ramshackle huts. Today, there are fifty thousand of them crammed into a small patch of land. Without running water or proper sewage facilities, the living conditions are appalling. Dehydration and dysentery are common among the children. There is a makeshift, erratic electrical supply to the slum, and little if any medical care available. Education is considered a luxury; many parents force their children to work almost from the time they can talk, in order to put one or two meals on the table every day.

Most of the people in Rasulpur are Muslims or Hindus. So it was not altogether surprising that at first, the team met with resistance. But Annamma and the team were not deterred. They gathered children who were roaming the alleyways and started a Balwadi (a nursery school). Since the parents could not afford to buy the children government school books, they let them go to Balwadi where they learned Telegu, Hindi, English, Maths, and Bible stories. Slowly the number attending increased. Today there are over one hundred regular attenders.

Gradually, Annamma and her team began meeting the needs of the older folk, who were beginning to accept the

---

is story is taken from a press release by Debbie Meroff of OM-ICT and *OM News* [summer 1997], p. 8.

presence of these strangers in their slum. Most of the illiterate adults in the slum were women. Their husbands, working as unskilled labourers, did not know from one day to the next if there would be any work for them and much of their erratic and scant income seemed to end up being used to purchase toddy, home-made liquor. As a result, many of the wives were left carrying the burden of providing for their families. These women often worked as maids in nearby middle-class homes.

The OM team started sewing classes with a professional teacher and encouraged slum women to join in the training for at least three hours a day. The team also began an adult literacy class. To this date, more than one hundred women have completed the sewing classes and have found employment in businesses around Hyderabad. Sixty people have similarly completed the adult literacy classes. They can now read the Bible in their own language! Part of this class is a Bible study during which time team members such as Annamma pray for the specific needs of the participants.

In the midst of this ministry of showing the love of Christ practically and compassionately, some of the slum dwellers started asking questions about why the team was doing this. Who was this god that Annamma was talking about? Why was he able to answer prayer when the team members came into their homes and prayed for their sick? Slowly people came to a small worship group meeting on Sundays. Today, an average of thirty-five people come to the worship services and 130 children to the Sunday School.

Sunday, September 29, 1996 was a big day for Annamma. On this day, twenty-one of her contacts publicly declared that Jesus was their Lord as they took jai dikhya. 'I could not believe my eyes,' Annamma said. 'I never expected that I would see the fruit of our ministry so soon. God has changed the lives of these people dramatically.'

Chandra, Swamy and their eldest son were three of the slum dwellers of Rasulpur baptised that day. It all began when Ba[...] their youngest son, announced to his mother who was wash[...] dishes outside their hut, 'I'm going to Sunday School. I lov[...]

singing and the story they are telling my friends.' Chandra didn't mind. Balu would be learning about God and good things in life. Chandra sighed. 'Where is God? My life is in a mess! What has God done for me?' She thought this way even though her husband was a priest who kept busy in the nearby temple.

Chandra was from a farming community in rural Andhra Pradesh. She had hoped that by marrying Swamy and moving to the big city, she would discover a better way of life. Instead the family ended up in Rasulpur, an illegal settlement on the edge of the airport. Slowly her dreams were shattered. Her eldest son had been taken into police custody recently, accused of murder. The police tortured him and harassed the family. They offered to release him if the family would pay a huge sum of money.

A few days after these traumatic events, the OM team had visited Chandra in her hut. The team members listened to her sad story and prayed with her. The next Sunday the team was surprised to see Chandra in the worship service. She explained: 'I was discouraged, but after you came to my house, I felt strengthened. I like praying to Jesus and listening to his teachings through my son, Balu. Things are changing in my life.'

That evening Swamy shouted at Chandra for going to the Christian worship service. 'This is not our god. What is wrong with our gods and goddesses? What about my profession?' The neighbours could hear Swamy shouting. Chandra decided to pray to this Jesus about her situation, as well as for her son in prison.

A short time later, the police suddenly released her son without Swamy having to pay any money. This event made such a positive impression on the family that the next Sunday the whole family was in the OM worship service. Then one by one they came to the saving knowledge of Jesus Christ.

This, then, is what in India we call a 'masala' taste (just a mixed taste!) of the incredible story of OM-India. It is a story almost unknown in the West. When Christians think of OM in the Western World, they usually think of our two ocean-going

Gospel ships, or short-term missions, or of our charismatic founder, George Verwer. Few realise that the largest ministry OM has worldwide is in India and that it is its most indigenised work globally. Yes, God is at work through nationals!

SEVEN

Moving Beyond Internationalising

Rob Sinclair epitomises what it means to be globalised. He is a Canadian who has spent fifteen of the last twenty-five years living in India. The interesting thing about Rob is that he is equally at home in free-spirited Vancouver, where he now resides with his family, as he is sitting cross-legged in a lungi (wrap-around skirt) on the dirt floor of a village home in Bihar, India drinking chai (Indian tea). Rob relates easily to the Chinese and Caucasian Canadians who come to his Vancouver home for a barbecue prior to the prayer meeting he holds there. He knows how to tell the latest Newfie joke (the equivalent of Irish jokes!), describe the esoteric joys of canoeing in the Rockies, and explain why real estate is so costly in Vancouver. Yet he is equally at ease telling the latest Sadaji jokes, speaking in Hindi, or being dressed in traditional Indian garb on the other side of the world. He also participates regularly in the Punjabi church in Surrey.

In 1996, Rob revisited India. He had been praying about leaving his present job to reassociate with OM-India, with whom he had laboured for many years. His main burden though was to see North India reached with the Gospel. Bihar in particular was on his heart. Historically this North Indian state of 87 million people (according to the 1991 census) had been so difficult a place to establish the church that it had been called 'the graveyard of missions'. Thus, he reacquainted himself with places in Bihar where he had taken OM evangelism teams two decades previously.

In one district (each district has about three million people) called Samastipur, Rob discovered that one of the only two evangelical churches was led by Lalit Paul who, it turned out, had received a tract from an OM team back in 1969, as the team had preached on the north shore of the Ganges River. Lalit was from Simri, a small village about 10 kilometres in from the road. He and his friend, Rabinlal Sahu, had sent for the free Bible correspondence course offered on the back of the tract. Through the disciplined study of God's Word, they had been saved and then baptised in the nearest church, in Samastipur.

Over the years Lalit's and Sahu's quiet witness had resulted in a number of other villagers from a Hindu background coming to faith in Christ, and in the forming of a small house church. Rob had known about this story and was seeking to encourage Lalit Paul during his trip across the state of Bihar. As he was sitting in Lalit's home, in walked Mohan Paul, also from the village of Simri. Upon being introduced, Mohan immediately exclaimed: 'We are the result of OM ministry.' He then told the story of coming to faith in Christ through the ministry of Lalit Paul and how other members of his family had come to Christ, including most recently his father – a big breakthrough. Rob's visit was a great encouragement to this small group of national, somewhat isolated Christians . It was only possible for one who could fit into two worlds as easily as a hand in a glove!

People who are bicultural or multicultural do not grow on trees! They are an increasingly valuable commodity in today's globalised world. Monocultural managers are a liability to international, jet-setting corporations. Worldly-wise managers are fought over. Kenichi Ohmae puts it this way, in relating biculturalism to how Japanese companies can get ahead globally: 'The best mediators are Japanese who have lived in the United States or another English-speaking country long enough to learn from personal experience how non-Japanese think, but not so long as to lose their identity as Japanese.'[1]

It is one thing to grow a multicultural person. But how do you grow a globalised organisation?! This is the dilemma that many multinational corporations face. And this is the issue we want to reflect on in this chapter as we continue to explore

---

[1] Kenichi Ohmae, *Beyond National Borders: Reflections On Japan and the World* (Homewood, IL: Dow Jones-Irwin, 1987), p. 106.

how globalisation impacts or should impact the world of missions.

The world economy is now being run by trading and manufacturing corporations, not nations. This fact alone should overcome any tendency toward isolation. A corporate worldview of isolation and monoculturalism is outmoded and regressive. The question remains, though, how do you measure 'globalisation'? At what point do you say that a company is globalised enough to function effectively in today's interdependent world? These questions are as much for mission as for secular organisations.

Globalisation of Mission Organisations

In the last several years, I have sought to test these questions in Operation Mobilisation. The fact that OM has been going through a corporate review has provided an impetus to this quest. As a result of that review seven key areas were identified where organisational growth and maturation were called for, in order for OM to remain vital. A new Mission Statement emerged from the evaluation:

> OM's role in the body of Christ is to motivate, develop and equip people for world evangelisation, and to strengthen and help plant churches, especially among the unreached in the Middle East, South and Central Asia, and Europe.

One of the seven key result areas in the plan of action called *Forward To 2001: A Plan For The Future Of Operation Mobilisation* is globalisation. OM has resolved the following in this growth area:

> We will go beyond being just international, striving for a truly multinational and transcultural partnership. This will enable each of our national entities to make a significant contribution to the movement in planning, decision making, strategising, and implementation. Internationally, we will not be dominated by any one country or

culture. Nationally, we will strive for substantial indigenisation in the leadership.

The other key result areas were: recruiting/mobilising, ministry training, people development and care, structures, world mission strategy, and resourcing and funding.

Under the globalisation key result area the goal set was: 'We will increasingly globalise the ethos, structures, and strategies of OM.' The objectives under the goal were:

1. Develop a plan for ongoing education in cultivating cross-cultural understanding and sensitivity and a global mindset.
2. Ensure that the diversity of OM is expressed in all international activities.
3. Commission a feasibility study regarding an international fund for support of workers from the new missionary-sending countries.
4. Establish in all fields a written policy on the use of the local language(s).

Further strategies were developed under the objectives.

But let's pause for a minute and consider. Why should such an international organisation (see chapter one) be fussing over globalisation so much? Hadn't OM already arrived in the internationalising process? Wasn't OM already globalised? To satisfy my own concerns about this issue, I conducted several surveys in 1993 and 1994 in OM. One was among our top hundred international leaders. Another survey undertaken (already referred to in chapter four) was among thirty Indian national leaders. A third was among a random sample of the seven hundred career missionaries in OM. Each survey addressed a different aspect of globalisation.

What the Grass Roots Are Saying About Globalisation

Early on in the research, a number of OMers from many different nationalities were asked open-ended questions about how 'globalised' they felt OM was. The comments were ver revealing. They suggested that OM might not be as globalised as it may imagine itself to be. Here are a few comments:

- There is not enough representation from the Two-Thirds World in important international decision-making groups. The West has the financial resources, operational techniques, and modern means of communication but is not learning enough from the Two-Thirds World in terms of their ways of training (real life oriented) or their spirituality borne out of a harder life-struggle. (Hong Kong OMer)
- [A] Western agenda still dominates. We have yet to find how to empower our leaders from the Two-Thirds World in international gatherings. (British OMer)
- It doesn't matter that you have people from all over the world [working with OM] if the way you act is on the basis of the Western World. (Argentinean OMer)
- We still focus so strongly on Western management and development styles and I always wonder if that is best. (Canadian OMer)
- [Globalisation] involves an inside change (is not just a matter of changing policy). (Argentinean OMer)
- Western dominance and arrogance run very deep, and will take many years before they will truly yield to real Third World leadership. (British OMer)
- There is a movement toward equal partnership but not far enough. (Singaporean OMer)

What the Experts Are Saying

A common theme in the grass-roots comments is that external and internal organisational realities may be two different things. That is to say, while externally, whether through policies or structures or whatever, an organisation may seem globalised, internally, in values and attitudes, the organisation may not model globalisation. For instance, the problem in OM, interpreted by anecdotal observations, is that, among some the members at least, there appears to be commendable globalisation going on, because there are so many nationalities represented and because OM works in so many countries. However, at the same time, the internal values and the organisational ethos are perceived to be favouring a Western World mindset, in the opinion of some of these people. Maturation in globalisation, then, would appear to occur when there is a consistency between the external and internal factors that together make up globalisation. Refer back to the definition of globalisation in chapter one, where this two-sided coin is said to represent true globalisation.

One of the problems in measuring globalisation (apart from the fact that its definition seems to involve a cluster of meanings, instead of being a simple and universally agreed upon definition) is that social scientists and management experts, in analysing multinational corporations or international organisations, use their own culture or companies with headquarters in their own country as their reference point, while they critique the globalisation of those same companies.[2] Nevertheless, there is a body of literature evolving which seeks to overcome the monocultural and ethnocentric approach to cross-cultural management research which characterises so much of it.[3]

Some cross-cultural management and social science researchers contend that strict comparison between different cultures is impossible, or difficult at best.[4] Ethnocentrism is perceived as a fundamental reason for such difficulties. *Random*

---

[2] Examples of this are Peter Senge, *The Fifth Dimension: The Art and Practice of the Learning Organization* (New York: Doubleday, 1990); Terrance E. Deal and Allan A. Kennedy, *Corporate Cultures: The Rites and Rituals of Corporate Life* (Reading, PA: Addison-Wesley, 1982); and Edgar Schein, *Organizational Culture and Leadership* (San Francisco: Jossey-Bass, 1992) which examine corporate culture from a very American perspective.

[3] Examples of this include all of K. Ohmae's books (quoted in earlier chapters); Nancy J. Adler, *International Dimensions of Organizational Behavior* (Boston: PWS-Kent, 1991); P. R. Harris and R. T. Moran, *Managing Cultural Differences* Houston: Gulf Publishing, 1987); and G. Hofstede, *Culture's Consequences: International Differences in Work-Related Values* (Beverley Hills, CA: Sage Publishers, 1984).

[4] For example, Marshall H. Segall, *Cross-Cultural Psychology: Human Behavior in Global Perspective* (Monterey, CA: Brooks/Cole, 1979), pp. 29–93, and A. R Negandhi, 'Comparative Management and Organization Theory: A Marriag Needed,' *Academy of Management Journal* 18(2): 334–343.

House Dictionary defines ethnocentrism as, 'Belief in the inherent superiority of one's own group and culture; it may be accompanied by feelings of contempt for those who do not belong; it tends to look down upon those considered as foreign; it views and measures alien cultures and groups in terms of one's own culture.' So what might be considered as selfish in one culture may be perceived as self-sacrificing in another. What might be perceived as an action that is consistent with human nature in one culture, may be considered as learned behaviour in the next. Cross-cultural experience opens people up to the different ways those of other cultures perceive things. However, as Glen Fisher argues, 'It takes considerable effort to override our habitual ways of perceiving and reasoning, to break out of established mindsets. . . . Our conscious selves . . . are not so much in charge as we think.'[5]

Similarly, studies in cross-cultural psychology support the thesis that there are less universal commonalties in human thought processes than most people think. This theory is supported, for instance, by Segall's findings on carpentering.[6] Through his experiment, Segall found that Westerners judge the diagonal on the left side of a Sander parallelogram as being longer than it really is. He explains this bias as being the result of a tendency to perceive a parallelogram drawn on a flat surface as a representation of a rectangular surface extended in space. This causes the viewer to judge the distance covered by the left diagonal as being greater than the distance covered by the right diagonal. This perception is seen as resulting from Western societies being highly 'carpentered.' That is to say, these societies are full of buildings with rectangular shapes. For those living in cultures where carpentered structures are a small part of the visual landscape, such as in Arab countries with their many domed mosques, inference habit of interpreting acute and obtuse angles as right angles extended in space is not as great. Through this 'Carpentered-World' hypothesis a generalisation is made that environment and culture shape our perceptual habits.

---

en Fisher, *Mindsets* (Yarmouth, ME: Sage Publishing, 1988), p. 25.
all, pp. *Cross-cultural Psychology*, 72–93.

On the other hand, some argue that there can be validity to findings when 'functional equivalence' is sought.[7] We might understand the sort of conceptual problem we are grappling with here by looking at an illustration probably familiar to the reader – the problem of Bible translation. A concern in Bible translation is that nothing is lost of the original sense of the words in the text (in Greek, Aramaic or Hebrew) in the process of translation. A loss of meaning can occur when too many liberties are taken with the actual words, so as to make the translation more of a paraphrase (or commentary!) as can be argued happened in the *Living Bible* and *Phillips* versions, but which enabled the Scripture to be readily understandable to the average person. Alternatively, too much emphasis may be placed on word-by-word translation so as to make a translation wooden or to undermine the sense of the actual thought, taken as a whole. Moreover, such an exact translation can fail to take into consideration the fact that some cultures may have no corresponding word in their language for the actual word used in the original. Dynamic equivalence, as understood by Bible translators, is concerned to ensure that the meaning of the text gets conveyed accurately across the language divide, whether or not it precisely involves a word-for-word translation.

Communication specialist, Fisher, reflects the basic position of those defending the viability of cross-cultural comparative studies when he says that, 'members of international communities share mutual assumptions regarding issues and a certain rationality, which reduce cross-cultural distance between them to a matter of little consequence.'[8] Hence, we might say that Fisher represents the 'dynamic equivalence' school of thought whereas Segall represents the strict (as in literal) translation school of thought!

---

[7] Examples are Gary J. Bekker and M. K. Taylor, 'Engaging the Other in the Global Village,' *Theological Education* 26(1) (Spring, 1990): 62–64; Nancy J. Adler, 'Typology of Management Studies Involving Culture,' *Journal of International Business Studies* (Fall, 1983): 43; M. Singer, *Intercultural Communication A Perceptual Approach* (Englewood Cliffs, NJ: Prentice-Hall, 1987), p. 75; and A. J. Row and R. O. Mason, *Managing With Style: A Guide to Understanding, Assessing, Improving Decision Making* (San Francisco: Jossey-Bass, 1989), pp. 138–158.

[8] Fisher, *Mindsets*, p. 68.

One of the most persuasive theories advanced along the 'dynamic equivalence' lines is by Childs.[9] He maintains that macro-level variables, such as organisational structures and technologies (e.g., computer systems), are becoming increasingly alike across cultures. Thus, according to this theory, ethnic culture is becoming a diminished variable in terms of things like organisational goals and values. For example, Pakistani managers in Lahore may want to make the company they work for as profitable as do their counterparts in London.

At the same time, Childs concludes, as a result of his research, that micro-level variables, most notably behaviour of employees in the work setting, are largely culturally determined and not corporately determined. Employees in Singapore may defer to the authority of their boss more than do their counterparts in Southampton, where it might be expected that decisions are made through consultation. Childs' research is not unique. Others who are extensively involved in cross-cultural organisational research have isolated significant diversity between managers of different cultures with respect to preferred styles of work behaviour, goals, and standards at the local level.[10] These variations found locally are often expressed in organisations in the form of different divisions that are assigned different work tasks or the creation of different products, as opposed to being for reasons of ethnicity.[11]

However, we can expect that in a mission organisation like OM, the main reason for diversity will be ethnicity. Hence ethnic culture remains a highly important variable in organisational culture when we're talking about globalisation in an organisation like OM. In other words, it should not be assumed that globalisation has not occurred if there remains a fair degree of diversity locally. On the other hand, if the local diversity exists without a strong and fairly uniform basic culture throughout the whole organisation, the organisation can

Cited in Adler, *International Dimensions*, 1983, p. 44.

B. M. Bass, P. C. Burger, R. Doctor, and G. V. Barrett, *Assessment: An International Comparison of Managers* (New York: The Free Press, 1979), pp. 176–186; ⸺ent and Hofstede in Adler, *International Dimensions*, 1991, pp. 42–58; ⸺n, *Organizational Culture*, pp. 259–262; Ohmae, *Triad Power*, 1985, p. 182. ⸺ein, *Organizational Culture*, pp. 264–272.

scarcely be said to be globalised and may be in danger of coming apart at the seams.

Part of the value of this sort of analysis is that it assumes that there are cultural differences which should not be ignored while making comparisons, but at the same time that one should not be paralysed by assuming that those differences are so profound as to render comparisons futile. This integrated approach to holding onto both universals and particulars in cross-cultural analysis is the method used in evaluating the degree of globalisation within OM.

Effective globalisation would exist in OM if there was universal consensus on vision and values (that is, if there was a shared corporate culture), but with preservation of local distinctives operating simultaneously. The assumption was made that regional or localised differences in themselves would not reflect a failure for OM as a whole in being globalised. Universals and particulars must coexist, the thesis defended, before globalisation can be said to have occurred. Failing that, what one would be left with is a surface form of internationalisation with one dominant culture. Or with an international organisation on the verge of breaking up because it was so fragmented.

Corporate or Organisational Culture

Just how important is corporate culture in the way an organisation functions, let alone in an international organisation? In management literature, recent theories have stressed the importance of such an in-house culture being fashioned if the company is to remain healthy as it moves from being a national entity to having an international presence. *Corporate or organisational culture* can simply be defined as 'the norms and values that shape behaviour in any organised setting.'[12] Organisational culture is formed in any organisation (Christian or

---

[12] Warren Bennis and Burt Nanus, *Leaders: The Strategies For Taking Cha*▪ (New York: HarperCollins Publishers, 1986), p. 111. Note that Bennis ▪ Nanus call this *social architecture*, but they make this expression synonyr▪ with *corporate culture*.

otherwise) through such activities as: story telling, rituals, traditions, symbols, styles of leadership, emphasis on relationship-building, the effect of behaviour as opposed to words, the language people use, the espoused mission statement, values and vision, the formalised principles and practices, and the definition of who the heroes are. For instance, in OM, great weight is given to the story of the beginnings of OM when three young people went to Mexico during their summer vacation to share the Gospel. Even though one of those three young people, George Verwer, OM's founder and international director, shares this story in many of his public meetings, whether they be in OM conferences or outside OM circles, the story doesn't seem to lose its magic. The story tells us that we (OMers) are people who are willing to take risks, emphasise faith living, work in teams, live simply, believe in sharing the Gospel with the unevangelised, work through nationals, and take on the hard places for God.

Edgar Schein uses an expanded definition of corporate or organisational culture which introduces us to the importance of this issue in globalisation matters. He says organisational culture is 'a pattern of shared basic assumptions that the group learned as it solved its problems of external adaptation and internal integration, that has worked well enough to be considered valid and, therefore, to be taught to new members as the correct way to perceive, think, and feel in relation to those problems.'[13] Lets apply the theory to our test case of OM: how successful has OM been in transferring the early values and vision to succeeding generations of OMers, and more specifically to the issue at hand, by those from Western World roots to

---

[13] Schein, *Organizational Culture*, p. 12. For other helpful explanations of the role of culture in an organisation's life see Stephen R. Covey's *Principle-Centered Leadership* (New York: Simon & Shuster, 1992); Deal and Kennedy's *Corporate Cultures*; Max Depree's *Leadership is an Art* (East Lansing, MI: Michigan State University Press, 1987); Burt Nanus' *Visionary Leadership* (San Francisco: Jossey-Bass Publishers, 1992); Rosabeth Moss Kanter's *The Change Masters* (New York: Simon & Shuster, Inc., 1984); A. M. Pettigrew's, 'On Studying Organizational Cultures,' *Administrative Science Quarterly* 22(4): 382–388; A. L. Wilkins' *Developing Corporate Character: How to Successfully Change An Organization Without Destroying It* (San Francisco: Jossey-Bass, 1989); and A. F. Harrison and R. M. Bramson's, *Styles of Thinking* (Garden City, NY: Anchor/Doubleday, 1982).

those from any number of other countries and continents? Do Indonesian OMers have the same sense of core values and underlying vision for the organisation that British OMers have?

All the relevant literature concurs that *vision* and *values* are integral to any meaningful understanding of 'how we do things around here,' that is, to how organisational culture works.[14] *Core values* answer the question: 'How do we want to act, in day-to-day life, in line with our mission statement, so as to achieve our vision?'.[15] *Vision* precedes *values* and is the answer to the question: 'What do we want to create?'.[16] Vision is shared, giving coherence to diverse activities, establishing an overarching corporate goal, whereby a common identity is established. Vision is long-term, a kind of organisational rudder. Values are short-term, like an navigational chart, as Stephen Covey would put it, helping people in day-to-day decision making and behaviour.

A Survey of OM's Core Values

With this conceptualisation in mind, a random survey of all OM missionaries was made concerning the official core values OM embraced and represented and by which it is characterised.[17] Those values are:

- knowing and glorifying God;
- living in submission to God's Word;
- being a people of grace and integrity;
- serving sacrificially;

---

[14] Wilkins, *Developing*, p. 33 Senge, *The Fifth Dimension*, pp. 181, 207–209; Deal and Kennedy, *Corporate Culture*, p. 21; Schein, *Organisational Culture*, pp. 17–20.
[15] Senge, *The Fifth Discipline*, p. 224; Fisher , Mindsets, p. 64; Schein, *Organisational Culture*, p. 151.
[16] Senge, *The Fifth Discipline*, p. 206.
[17] A complete list of who these people are is found in OM's annually-produced *Personnel* booklet. The 1994 version was used for the purposes referred herein. Since a polling of OMers had been conducted in 1993 to discern w consensus there was concerning OM core values, as part of the OM corpe review, the results of which led to the official list of core values from whic survey was taken, the goal was not to discover what the organisation values were, but to compare views on values across cultures.

- loving and valuing people;
- reflecting the diversity of the Body of Christ;
- evangelising the world;
- interceding globally;
- esteeming the church.

Each respondent was asked to rank the core values from one to nine in terms of how he or she considered them to be important to him or herself. Variables considered in the analysis were gender, length of service in OM, nationality.

The results of the survey revealed that the two groups of Two-Thirds Worlders and Westerners are very similar in the way they view the core values: six of the core values were ranked in the same order by the two groups.

Of all the core values, 'reflecting the diversity of the Body of Christ' would be the value most closely corresponding to globalisation. The subtitle of this core value in OM's manual *Forward to 2001* is 'International team living – globalisation'. All OMers have a copy of this manual and so had been able to ponder the meaning of the core values for themselves, even if their ministry might have kept them so isolated from the OM mainstream that they had been unable to participate in the process of the corporate review which had taken place prior to the conducting of the survey and which was referred to earlier. One could therefore conclude from the survey results that the two groups viewed globalisation in much the same way, in terms of their understanding of its degree of importance in the OM scheme of things.

Another way to interpret the significance of the differences between Two-Thirds World and Western World OMer views on core values is to introduce other factors into the analysis. When short-term versus long-term service[18] and male versus female variables are introduced, it is apparent that geography is less a factor than gender or length of service! Of the three variables considered, length of service in OM influences perception the most, that is, the way of viewing OM and one's

---

ording to OM definitions, *short-term* refers to a period of service not ng two years, and *long-term* to any tenure in OM exceeding two years. g-termers in OM are, in effect, career missionaries.

place in it. Intercultural consensus over which core values are most important suggests that OM has been relatively successful in socialisation across cultures; there is a global sense of what the organisation stands for in the way of vision and values. The high degree of consistency in comparing responses of Two-Thirds World participants with Western World participants indicates that OM has forged a common organisational culture. A biopsy of this aspect of the OM body shows a healthy extent of globalisation. How else, though, can we test for globalisation in missions, using OM as a case study? Is there some way we can check the accuracy of the results from the findings of this survey?

Styles of Leadership Throughout OM

To cross-check the validity of the above findings, a survey was conducted among the top leaders of OM, assessing leadership styles between cultures. If the degree of globalisation had been overrated, it was suspected, there would be little cross-over in styles of leadership when comparing leaders from the Two-Thirds World with leaders from the Western World, if a standard basis of measurement of styles were to be used in the analysis. That is to say, if globalisation were to occur anywhere in the organisation, one could expect that it would occur among its top executives. If, however, major differences in decision-making styles could be proved to exist on the basis of nationality (that is, on the basis of whether one was from the Two-Thirds World or the Western World) then it would surely suggest that OM had not penetrated very far in its globalisation efforts. With this idea in mind, an instrument was chosen to test the style of decision making employed by the various leaders who make up OM's International Leaders' Group (ILG), a select body of the top hundred or so leaders in OM. Alan Rowe's and Richard Mason's Decision Style Inventory (DSI), as outlined in their book, *Managing With Style: Guide To Understanding, Assessing, and Improving Decision Making*, was employed to survey the range of styles across cultures.

Care was taken at the outset to ascertain whether the instrument used to measure styles of decision making among leaders (the DSI) would have any validity across cultures; it had been primarily used to measure leadership styles of management in American companies or multinational corporations with American roots and/or an international headquarters based in the United States. Bearing in mind what was said above about the difficulty of measuring something interculturally, there was, nevertheless no other instrument available that had such widespread cross-cultural exposure or validification in comparing leadership styles. With its philosophical roots in Jungian psychology whereby four basic personality types were identified, regardless of race or culture (assumed to be universally valid)[19], and later honed through the Myles Briggs Type Indicator, the DSI maintains that: 'There is something programmed within us, deep in the recesses of our minds, that causes us to view the world in different ways and to react accordingly ... [so that] there are discernible patterns of style [decision making] that occur over and over again in the general population.'[20]

Four basic styles provide the conceptual framework for the way people think and decide, thus giving meaning to the differences in behaviour we observe in everyday life. While the DSI becomes a useful management tool because it furnishes a means of measuring style and of bringing specificity to the language of decision style, it was felt that in an international context (like OM) it might also serve the purpose of exposing congruence or incongruence in styles of decision making on the basis of culture (nationality). Based on my previous experience of nine years attendance at the annual leaders' meetings to which those in the International Leaders' Group (ILG) came, it was my hunch prior to conducting the test among these OM leaders, that the international style of conducting business

---

[9] Anthropologist Ralph Linton concluded, on the basis of his research, that
  ere is considerable range of variation in personality types within given soci-
  ·s and much the same personality types present in all societies so that 'when
  becomes sufficiently familiar with an alien culture and the individuals
  share it, one finds that these individuals are fundamentally the same as
  ·s people he has known in his own society' *The Cultural Background of
  ·lity* (New York: Appleton-Century-Crofts, Inc., 1945), pp. 148–149.
  · and Mason, *Managing with Style*, p. 19.

meetings, the way decisions were made, etc. favoured a Western World mindset and customs. In other words, if what Rowe
and Mason say was true – preferred styles of decision making
are innate and not learned – we could expect to see a congruence of styles in OM internationally, regardless of the nationality of the leader. Lack of congruence would suggest either that
the organisation is not as globalised as it thought, or that the
style of leadership is culturally determined; conditioning
would then prevail over conception, nurture over nature. The
implication of this latter finding would be that an international
organisation must seek a way to accommodate the various
leadership styles in order to truly function in a globalised sense.

The DSI was handed out and explained to the 94 leaders
attending the ILG meetings in Mosbach, Germany in January,
1994. These were CEO or middle-management type leaders. All
were fluent in English.

The data were organised in several ways. First of all, a com-
posite profile for the organisation was developed, based on
searching for the average score for all the surveys, and then
comparing that with the typical score of DSI respondents in
general as determined by Rowe and Mason.[21] Then comparisons were made between Two-Thirds World and Western
World mean scores, a determination made of the range in the
data overall, an examination done of the mode overall, and a
comparison made of the styles of decision making on the basis
of gender.

Interestingly enough, the findings indicated that there was
little difference in style of decision making between Westerners
and non-Westerners. The most common Two-Thirds World
style was what Rowe and Mason would label a *behavioural-
directive* style, found in 28.5 per cent of the cases (there are
numerous possible combinations of leadership styles). On the
other hand, the most popular Western World leadership style
was the *behavioural-conceptual* style, representing 22.6 per cent o͡
their population. Note that the *behavioural* trait was tʰ
dominant one in both sets of leaders. Such a finding is ɾ

---

[21] It is beyond the limits of this book to explain how the DSI 'scientif
works but a thorough explanation is given in Rowe and Mason's textbͦ

insignificant! A closer examination of the data revealed that the main difference between the two sets of OM leaders was that the Two-Thirds World leaders were more analytical and less conceptual than their Western World counterparts. Both were similar when it came to being directive and behavioural.

What qualities are characteristic of those with *behavioural* strengths? This is the most people-oriented of the four styles. Leaders with this style are receptive to suggestions, show warmth, use persuasion, focus on short-term problems, and are action oriented. Each person has a combination of preferred styles of decision making whereby one style could be 'very dominant' (almost always used and is characteristic of 16 per cent of the population), one could be 'dominant' (found in 15 per cent of the general population and used much of the time), one could be a 'backup' style (found in 38 per cent of the population and reverted to in making decisions occasionally), and one could be a 'least preferred' style (found in 31 per cent of the population and rarely used in making decisions).

Clearly OM either socializes leaders to adopt this pastoral-type leadership style or seeks out leaders (consciously or unconsciously) who will fit a right brain, corporate leadership profile which the behavioural style represents. OM's preferred style of leadership certainly is not typical of the average executive tested by Rowe and Mason. Their findings reveal that the classic profile of an executive is *conceptual-directive*. That is, the conceptual style is dominant or very dominant and the directive approach is either of dominant or backup strength. *Conceptual* characteristics in decision making are: creativity, the possession of a broad outlook, impatience with rules, independence, intuitiveness, and being feeling-oriented. *Directive* qualities are: practicality, predilection to structure, stress on the 'here and now', decisiveness, and being results-focused. *Analytical* qualities include being idealistic, being extremely nalytical, being self-disciplined, being autocratic, and being chnically oriented.

ooking at the data another way, the mean of each of the styles for the OM Two-Thirds World leaders was 74.93 for directive styles, 79.07 for analytical, 74.4 for conceptual, 4 for behavioural. Typical scores for each style in the general population are 75 for directive (almost the same as above), 90 for analytical (the OM Two-Thirds Worlders are well below the mean), 80 for conceptual (lower than the mean), and 55 for behavioural (well above the mean). So while there are some consistencies with universal findings on preferred leadership styles, with the directive style showing congruence, there are some more than subtle differences in the conceptual category, and significant differences in the analytical and behavioural ones. OMers are not typical leaders.

Discrepancies between the two groups of OM leaders become accentuated when open-ended responses are factored into the analysis. Below are just a few of the many fascinating responses to the DSI.

- Too frank and too 'I' centred. It [the survey] should be more in relation to culture, family, or group. (Singaporean)
- In our culture we never analyse ourselves to this extent. (Indian)
- They [the questions] are too blunt and direct. (Malaysian)
- The mentality [of Western superiority] has not changed. We must not stop at lip service [in globalisation]. (Filipino)
- The need for Two-Thirds World leaders [in OM] to be fluent in English . . . does not ensure their full participation in the discussion. (Malaysian)
- We need to encourage more [participation in the ILG meetings] from the non-vocal ones who are from the Two-Thirds World. A lot of the Two-Thirds World people are sometimes not vocal because they are afraid of [expressing] contrary opinion, which might affect their funding, which at times comes largely from the developed countries. (Indian)

What can be concluded from this data? Firstly, OM does have preferred leadership style internationally. This consistency leadership styles is indicative of a solid degree of globalisa in the organisation. Secondly, there are enough differenc the styles between the two groups to suggest that one ap to decision making could dominate the other. When you take that fact into consideration with the wide-ranging comments on globalisation by OM leaders, particularly from the Two-Thirds World, you would tend to conclude that OM is not as globalised as it appears to be. For instance, the approach to decision making in business meetings favours Westerners. Could it be that Childs' theory is being borne out here? That is to say, we are dealing at the ILG level in OM with top executive decision making (macro level), which explains the commonality of leadership traits, but when digging under the surface, significant differences are found (more at the micro level). The question is: Who has to adjust to whom? On the basis of the informal comments made in response to the questionnaire conducted, a selection of which are recorded above, it is my opinion that the Two-Thirds World leaders in OM have had to do much more of the adjusting to the Western World side than vice versa. Is that reflective of true globalisation?

A recent study conducted by the business consulting firm Arthur Andersen of the United States called *East Meets West – The Changing Faces of Management*, involved 1,721 senior executives from the Pacific Rim, Germany, France, Britain and the United States. It shows some differences in the way senior Western managers work in relation to their Eastern counterparts. The Western style of management is described as being more flexible, creative, open, direct and confrontational, whereas the Asian style is likely to be paternalistic, putting greater value on seniority, relationships and family ties. The thesis here is that these differences blur, the longer a person functions in a cross-cultural or multicultural context.

Hellrigel and Slocum have found that differences in styles of decision making and personality are not synonymous, so leaders and managers tend to adjust their styles to an integration of the four Jungian psychological types.[22] Similarly, Rowe and

---

[22] Those types are ST (sensing/thinking), NT (intuiting/thinking), SF (sensing/feeling), and NF (intuiting/feeling). It is well worth noting the four DSI leadership styles of directive, analytical, conceptual, and behavioural closely follow the Jungian typology. See D. Hellriegel and J. W. Slocum, 'Managerial Problem-Solving Styles', *Business Horizons*. December, 1975, pp. 29–37 for details of the research based on Jungian psychological types.

Mason in their DSI research found that most successful executives exhibit both left and right brain styles, leading one to believe that within an organisation like OM the sort of leader who will succeed is someone who has demonstrated a capacity to use both a technical-logical style (left brain= analytical and directive styles) and a people-oriented-creative-integrative style (right brain= conceptual and behavioural styles). Certainly at the international level, a synthesis of styles allows for smoother co-operation, and to the extent that there is a congruence of styles in a rather large decision-making body (like the ILG), those present will feel more or less comfortable and able to achieve consensus on the various issues facing them.

Recent leadership theory supports the thesis that good leaders learn to adjust their style to the demands of the situation, ranging from a task-oriented approach to a relation-oriented approach. Flexible leadership styles are being promoted as viable, indeed necessary, even within monocultural companies. This has been called, 'situational leadership' by Hershey and Blanchard.[23] How much more then can we expect to see this adjustable leadership style emerge interculturally as ethnocentricism among leaders? This question gets sent lead-weighted to the ocean floor!

Is an international organisation like OM globalised? Yes and no! Let's probe deeper into this complexity in the next chapter. Do we need all this probing? In a day and age when the Two-Thirds World church is jumping on the band wagon of world evangelisation and wanting to partner in meaningful ways with the Western World church (such as through mission agencies like OM) dare we look at the implications of these developments in a surface way only? To ensure that we 'do it right', we need to thoroughly understand the dynamics of the two solitudes being fused. To be forewarned is to be forearmed! What do we need to understand about each other, then, in order to function together effectively?

---

[23] Paul Hershey and Kenneth H. Blanchard, *Management of Organizational Behavior: Utilizing Human Resources* sixth ed. (Englewood Cliffs, NJ: Prentice Hall, 1993). Chapters 4 and 5 of their book offer a good overview of twentieth-century leadership theory. Chapter 5 focuses on those who espouse the situational leadership school of thought.

EIGHT

Transformation from the Inside Out

Statistics often tell a story. I discovered that 38 per cent of those who completed the OM core values survey intimated that they felt OM was insufficiently globalised. Among the top international leaders in OM, 68 per cent of those who responded to the question 'Do you feel there is an equal partnership between the Western World and Two-Thirds World sides of OM?' replied, 'No'. This raised several questions: What accounted for that large degree of dissatisfaction when there was such widespread agreement between cultures on what OM's core values ought to be? Furthermore, what accounted for the similarity among OM leaders in their leadership styles, regardless of nationality, when those leadership styles were not typical of leadership styles of the general population – unless the similarity could be seen as a function of successful globalisation? Hence, if OM is so globalised, why the undercurrent of criticism about Westernisation?

Certain comments tell a story, too. At one of our international gatherings, a veteran OMer told me that she felt, 'OM is still very Anglo-Saxon in orientation . . . with very few Westerners becoming like Indians, although they are becoming like us.' Is the socialisation to OM core values and ethos and vision a movement of Orientals to Occidentals, or of opposites toward each other? The above comment suggests that non-Westerners are perceived as having to do most of the adjusting in OM. Another off-hand observation by an Argentinean OM leader shows the impression some have about the direction in which the training and socialisation are heading. He exclaimed: 'In some ways, OM across cultures does share a common method to prepare missionaries in a complete way, but it is more of an American or European type of training.' Again, the adjustment is viewed as being somewhat one-directional, from East to West.

There is no question that OM is highly internationalised, as measured in terms of the number of nationalities working with it from all major regions of the world. OM has also succeeded in placing nationals in charge of many of its front-line ministries and all national entities are well represented at their global gathering. Moreover, there is evidence of a strong organisational culture across the OM world: an indication of globalisation. Such realities may be present in many other international mission societies. Then what accounts for the paradox? Let's do some further investigation and analysis.

Making Relationships Primary

If there is one aspect of globalisation that everyone seems to agree is an essential ingredient to make it work, it is intercultural, relationship building. As Dodd maintains, 'Effective intercultural communication begins with a recognition that a focus on task alone is insufficient.'[1] There has already been some reflection about the importance of relationship building in chapters two and three, when considering the theological framework for embracing globalisation.

OM has long cherished relationships within the organisation as being crucial components to understanding what OM is. It has always grabbed at my heart strings in meetings when George Verwer declares: 'You are not joining a movement, you are the movement!' Out of his regular exhortations to work at building healthy interpersonal relationships with our missionary colleagues came his book *Revolution of Love*. A people-centred approach to ministry has been modelled by George himself. He has always had time for the rank and file in OM. George is not an inaccessible leader even though he leads

---

[1] C. H. Dodd, *Dynamics of Intercultural Change* (Dubusque, IA: W. C. Brown, 1987), p. 33.

an organisation of thousands of missionaries. During the seven years I was outside the organisation, George kept in personal contact with me better than anyone else in OM. His high-touch leadership had a lot to do with my wife and me deciding to return to OM some years ago.

On a trip I had to make to England in April, 1998, he carved time out of his hectic schedule to take me on a two-hour walk in the lovely Kent spring countryside, simply because I had let him know I was passing through London and would appreciate having a few minutes with him.

George's letters or cellular phone calls out of the blue to a wide range of OM alumni and supporters worldwide are legendary. This orientation has permeated down through the ranks of OM and partially explains why so many Two-Thirds World friends of OM have been drawn to more a formal association.

As mentioned earlier, many Two-Thirds World cultures are people oriented. The scanty missiological literature on globalisation generally concurs that relationship or friendship building is crucial for any meaningful sense of equal partnership to emerge interculturally.[2] For example, as Fisher has documented, Latin Americans place less emphasis on managing things or programmes than they do on managing relationships.[3] To make Latins feel at home in a Western-based mission agency, then, one would expect that a high emphasis would be placed on the nurturing of affirmative interpersonal relationships. This may not be easy with personality types or people from cultures where there is a strong task orientation. So, for example, when an organisation brings co-workers together for international conferences or global strategy meetings, it makes sense to be less business-like than other organisations might be by building good doses of leisurely time for one-to-one type of relating, and small group sessions into the programme. Trust is nurtured in Two-Thirds World cultures by spending quality time with people. This is increasingly becoming a felt need in secularised, technological Western society, but the

[2] Samuel and Corwin, *EMQ.*, Kraakevik and Welliver, *Partners*; Taylor, 1991; and 1994; Sookhdeo, *New Frontiers*.

[3] Fisher, *Mindsets*, p. 54.

accent is still on building trust in the West through proven competency.[4] Nevertheless, organisations seeking to globalise should pay heed to Dodd's advice: 'By the nature of the process, intercultural communication is rooted in the social relationships that accompany our actions ... [so that] our relationship with the person with whom we are communicating affects how the message is interpreted.'[5]

Another area where the differences between task-oriented and people-oriented cultures should be respected is regarding the greater personal attention and loyalty displayed by people-oriented cultures toward their family members.[6] While acknowledging that I am generalising, it has been my observation that OMers who I have worked with from Two-Thirds World countries have faced more pressure from back home than their Western World counterparts. Rather than making one policy across the board for things like retirement funds, home leave, and furlough (home assignment), generally emanating out of Western missionary society practice, greater latitude should be given by international organisations to workers from cultures where there is greater reverence for family. Showing personal concern and flexibility interculturally in such ways engenders loyalty and better productivity. Escobar summarises the importance of putting people ahead of programmes when he says: 'Fellowship is interrelated with mission, relationship precedes function, friendship precedes efficiency.'[7]

Even secular management theorists have increasingly come to recognise that such user-friendly approaches to management are good for business. Deal and Kennedy, for instance, stress the integral role relationship building has in effecting corporate consensus, whether that be to sell massive change internally or to branch out into selling new products.[8] Consulting those affected by the change prior to initiating the

---

[4] Elmer, *Conflict* p. 179.

[5] Dodd, *Dynamics*, pp. 27, 33.

[6] John Maxwell, 'The Asian Way of Doing Business – Is It Really Any Different?' *Silver Kris* (January, 1994): 30.

[7] Escobar, speech 1991.

[8] Deal and Kennedy, *Corporate Cultures*, p. 164.

change is one example of how this people-friendly approach works. Bennis and Nanus call this style of management 'collegial' as opposed to 'hierarchical'. A collegial style of leadership sees decision making as participative and 'bottom-up', whereby everyone has a chance to contribute ideas that eventually lead to consensus around the issues.[9] Not only Two-Thirds Worlders but Westerners want to feel that they are being treated as real people in the organisations for which they work. As John Gardener says in his inspirational book on leadership, 'Wise leaders are continuously finding ways to say to their constituents, "I hear you." '[10] Stephen Covey speaks of it in terms of building up emotional dividends with people, dividends which leaders can cash in later, but which stem from truly listening to people on their own terms, respecting their point of view, etc.[11] Yes, if secular theorists can recognise the integral role relation building has in effective organisational life, then let's smarten up in mission circles!

Cultivating Common Vision and Values

The movement of contemporary organisations tends to be centrifugal. What does this mean? It means that there are more forces at work to pull the organisation apart than there are to pull it together! This is especially true of an international entity which seeks to preserve a corporate identity in the face of regional differences. It is what John Naisbitt calls 'the global paradox.' He says that ironically at the same time as we are being forced to think globally – economically or electronically, 'tribalism' increases. He defines *tribalism* as 'the belief in fidelity to one's own kind, defined by ethnicity, language, culture, religion, or, in the late twentieth century, profession.'[12] We only have to read our newspapers to see that, literally, tribalism is active as never before. In the Balkans, Serbs war against

---

Bennis and Nanus, *Leaders*, pp. 120–121.

John Gardener, *On Leadership* (Toronto: MacMillan Canada Inc., 1993), p. 27.

See his chapter entitled 'Paradigms of Interdependence' in *The 7 Habits of ~ly Effective People* (New York: Simon & Shuster, Inc., 1990).

~isbitt, 1995, p. 20.

Muslims. In Iraq, Arabs war against Kurds. In India, Sikhs want separation to form their own country. As these words are penned, there is much furore in Canada because the French government is planning to issue a stamp commemorating General Charles De Gaulle's infamous state visit to Canada in the 1960s when he inflamed the passions of Quebecois separatists with his now-famous line, 'Vive le Quebec, libre.' Yes, ironically, as English becomes the lingua franca globally, everyone's mother tongue becomes more and more a passionate issue for the individual. And so in the Common Market-driven Europe, Great Britain has put up a long-standing resistance to the introduction of the euro.

How then do we heal wounds in the midst of such stitch-popping diversity? Obviously, a certain amount of attention must be given by the international organisation to cultivating common vision and values right across the board. Furthermore, this shaping and reinforcing of universal corporate vision and values in missions must come as a result of 'thoughtful, mutual listening... from every tradition and culture because the world-wide church is indispensable for mission.'[13] Only in such interaction can the ethnocentricity of parochialism give way to the universally shared values that will be representative of a truly globalised mission around which a common vision will be shared. These universally held values and vision must not only be held by those in the top leadership echelons but must also percolate down to and from the grass roots of the organisation.

In a group like OM, care must be taken to ensure that strategic planning exercises, efforts at standardising training materials, and the putting on of international conferences receive proper input from the disparate sides of the organisation, not just from the nationalities which are quick to speak up and prone to reveal feelings without embarrassment. If it is true that 'the squeaky wheel gets the grease', then it behoves Western World partners in the global arrangement to bite their tongues more frequently so that those who do not speak up easily will have their voices heard once in a while! Those less out-spoken just happen to b⸱

---

[13] V. Ramachandra, 'The Honor of Listening: Indispensable for Mission,' *EN* 30(4): 405.

the newcomers to the world missions scene – our friends from the Two-Thirds World!

Cultivating a Milieu of Cultural Sensitivity

Organisations like OM need to face up to the fact that their historic roots are Western. This reality has prejudiced such organisations in their ability to be aware of their own ethnocentricity. In other words, such mission organisations don't seem to realise how Westernised they really are! Let's look at a few of the specific areas where assumptions are made about how international organisations should function which predispose the organisation to choose a Western mindset over an Eastern mindset. We admit that generalisations and characterisations are being made here which may not always be true. To cite one example, based on a generalisation made above: the Swiss may not be as outspoken as their German and British fellow Europeans, who may not be as assertive as their American cousins – all of whom nevertheless get painted with the same broad stroke brush as being 'Westerners'. James Plueddemann, missions' executive and educator, makes an interesting case for claiming that major cultural differences are less and less related to the East-West bipolarity, and more and more to rural-urban, industrial-agricultural, or the amount of formal education categories.[14] Nonetheless, enough cultural dissimilarity is manifested, especially between Western World and Two-Thirds World peoples, to make such comparisons basically valid.

As we enter this section, it is also helpful to preface the analysis with a definition of *culture*. The Willowbank Report, sponsored by the Lausanne Committee for World Evangelisation in 1978, in its summarising of the consultation on 'Gospel and Culture', stated that, 'Culture is a term not easily susceptible of definition'. Consistent with the thrust of the Willowbank Report's findings on culture is Paul Hiebert's definition of

---

ulture, Learning and Missionary Training,' in Taylor, *Internationalising
g*, 1991, pp. 217–230.

culture as 'the integrated system of learned patterns of behaviour, ideas, and products characteristic of a society.'[15] This understanding will be used in this book.

Aspects of cultural sensitivity

1. Time. In time-oriented cultures, careful use of time is associated with reward. Punctuality in time-oriented cultures is valued. So are tightly-scheduled, goal-directed activities. History and dates are important. Devices that enhance such efficient use of time such as day planners, pocket calculators and computers are considered indispensable tools. In contrast, in event-oriented cultures, the event, or activity, or association with the people involved in the event or activity, is the reward. Delays (as perceived by the time-oriented person) in starting and concluding scheduled meetings are viewed as normal and acceptable. The present is more relevant than the future or the past.[16]

Little wonder then that I misread the situation and faced considerable frustration when I first arrived in India and discovered people showing up for the church services fifteen to thirty minutes late! I soon came to learn that only unimportant guests show up on time!

Studies reveal that Americans tend to be at the extreme end of a continuum in being time-oriented, with Koreans being slightly more event-oriented than time-oriented, and Latins being at the other end of the continuum, in being extremely event-oriented.[17] Even among time-oriented, or event-oriented cultures, there are variations in the use of time.[18] For example,

---

[15] Quoted in Arthur Glasser, 'The Missionary Task.' in Arthur Glasser, Paul Hiebert, Peter Wagner, and Ralph Winter, eds. *Crucial Dimensions of World Evangelization* (Pasadena, CA: William Carey Library, 1976), p. 45. For a good definition of *culture* see also Eugene Nida, *Customs and Culture* (Pasadena, CA: William Carey Library, 1979), p. 28.

[16] Sherwood G. Lingenfelter and Marvin K. Mayers, *Ministering Cross-Culturally: An Incarnational Model for Personal Relationships*, (Grand Rapids MI: Baker Book House, 1991), pp. 37–51; E. T. Hall, *The Hidden Dimension* (Garden City, NY: Doubleday, 1966), p. 124.

[17] Lingenfelter and Mayers, pp. 49–50.

[18] E. T. Hall, *The Silent Language* (Garden City, NY: Doubleday, 1 pp. 170–180.

monochronic cultures do one thing at a time. Anthropologists have found that North American cultures tend to be monochronistic;[19] Latin and Arabic cultures, on the other hand, are *polychronic*. They are comfortable doing several things at once, while the monochronic person looking on feels that the situation is chaotic. Numerous other distinctions can be made about the way people from various cultures organise their value and behavioural systems around time.

How important it is, then, to be sensitive to one another in intercultural settings. It is quite one thing to say how a church meeting should function in Timbuktu when you are from Toronto, and quite another thing to say how a meeting should function when you are one of twenty nationalities present from four different continents in a setting where each one of those present has the same reason for being there. In the former case, surely it would be appropriate to adopt the attitude of, 'When in Rome do as the Romans do' (unless some clear biblical principle is being violated), whereas in the latter setting (typical of an international mission gathering) there ought to be some accommodation made for the preferences of the various participants. We'll come back to this discussion in chapter ten on contextualisation and globalisation.

2. *Formality*. Some cultures are relatively informal. I realise that, in being a Canadian, I am perceived by much of the world, including by my ancestors – the English – as being far too informal. Yet even I sometimes cringe when faced with what I consider to be the extreme informality (to the point of rudeness – by my way of looking at things), of some Americans. Other cultures are highly formal, whether in terms of relationships or adherence to the law. The British may be reticent, to some extent, to wear their hearts on their sleeves, but they are downright forthright and frank in comparison to the inscrutable Chinese.[20] For the Westerner, nationalities like the Japanese are hard to fathom because in face-to-face relations formalities and protocol are maintained, no matter how

---

[19] E. T. Hall, *Beyond Culture* (Garden City, NY: Anchor, 1976), pp. 16–20.
[20] Lingenfelter and Mayer, *Ministering Cross-Culturally*, pp. 106–107.

one is feeling, making it difficult to measure the dynamics of a meeting accurately. What is going on in this setting is a clash between what E. T. Hall describes as *high-context* and *low-context* societies.[21]

According to Hall, people raised in a high-context culture expect that participants in a given situation will be highly skilled in perceiving what is going on internally, even though externally, through such things as conversation, nothing conclusive is discernible. To expect the crucial piece of the puzzle to fall into place explicitly or openly is to insult the other party and is considered to be a personal violation. Causing someone in a group setting to 'lose face' is thus considered to be the unpardonable sin. You don't even do that to your worst enemy in some high-context societies.

Koreans would be an example of those coming from high-context cultures. Thus, it is important for a Korean to be able to 'read' someone's feelings or thoughts from their facial gestures. For them, to say 'no' may mean 'yes', depending on the non-verbal communication going on. The Korean who sees an English lady speak her mind frankly might be evidence to the Korean that the outspoken lady is proud, whereas an American may admire her forthrightness and think she is honest. Feelings are not expressed directly in a high-context society.

Patrick Sookhdeo pinpoints the importance of Westerners distinguishing between the *private face* and the *public face* in dealings with those from the Two-Thirds World and observes that, 'In some cultures, good interpersonal relationships take precedence over competence and efficiency [and]to get along with a person with the minimum of friction is more important than the rate at which the job is done.'[22] Such nuances of intercultural relating will not be experienced unless Westerners are educated about the differences between high-context and low-context cultures. Instead, Two-Thirds Worlders, as usual, will have to adjust their ways to the Western customs.

---

[21] Hall, *Beyond Culture*, 1976, pp. 57, 142.
[22] 'Cultural Issues in Partnership in Mission,' in Taylor, *Kingdom Partnerships*, 1994, pp. 59–60.

3. *Territoriality.* We often associate the concept of territory with animal behaviour. Who has not seen a dog mark out the invisible line of its territory by barking when any stranger reaches a certain point in approaching its master's house? Dogs will even determine territory by urinating in certain places so that other dogs get the message that a particular space is theirs! But humans also define their use of space.[23] Just as with the use of time and in matters of formality, little is communicated verbally when expectations differ within a group, yet associations with and feelings about the use of space remain powerful[24] For example, Latins do not require much separate space and so will crowd (by a Swede's viewpoint) the 'private space' of someone he or she is talking to. In spite of their British ties through colonialism, Indians jump queues with abandon. It is called survival of the fittest when you go to the Bombay railway station to join the many others queing up to make train reservations – particularly as you get closer to the ticket window. But heaven forbid, if you try that in Great Britain! Similarly, while Americans make their homes their castles, they are somewhat casual and informal about others entering their private space, whereas in Germany it would be considered by many Germans as an affront for an uninvited person to enter a private room. These are but a few examples of the notion of territoriality which is culturally determined. As missionaries enter new cultures, they can learn territoriality informally, but better pre-field education can overcome some of the culture shock and any faux pas made in the course of cross-cultural living and communication of the Gospel.

How does territoriality work within an international organisation as members relate to each other while being from different cultural backgrounds? A person might have decades of experience working in the Turkish world, but that does not mean they know how to relate effectively to a Korean colleague working alongside them. Incidentally, with Koreans coming in waves to the 10–40 Window, we need to do some homework on how to relate respectfully to people from that xenophobic

---

Hall, *The Silent Language*,1959, pp. 188–205.
Hall, *The Hidden Dimension*, 1966, pp. 8–15, 124–128.

background. We should not expect that all the adjustment be made by them to us! A suggestion was made by a Chinese missionary in OM that when OMers come together annually for leaders' meetings, Westerners would help Easterners to open up verbally more in the plenary meetings by arranging the chairs differently. She pointed out that sitting people in a traditional classroom fashion encouraged formality and meant that the speaker or chairperson should not be interrupted or disagreed with, even if that person welcomed feedback or input. To arrange chairs in a circle or semi-circle, on the other hand, she said, would signal to the Chinese that they not only had a right but a duty to speak their minds, although still with a great deal of deference to the one in charge of the meeting. There had been criticism at the reluctance of Two-Thirds World participants to speak out in these sessions, even though they had been publicly encouraged to do so. Space, apparently, was having a profound influence on their ability to feel sufficiently at ease to risk venturing into public communication. As we shall see later, other issues were also involved in this reluctance to speak out.

4. *Organisation.* There are various aspects to the establishing of an organising pattern in any given culture. Three of the predominant ones are *order*, *selection* and *congruence*.[25] Major differences exist between cultures over things concerning *order* such as chronology of birth in a family, arrival sequence at a meeting, and number and order of courses to be served at a meal. For instance, in an Indian society, the eldest son will have certain familial responsibilities that the second son will not have. Whereas in an American family, order of birth is often irrelevant to developing a sense of duty to parents or family. Once during a visit to a Tamil pastor, whom I had not seen for many years, his mother suddenly died. He and the church had gone to great lengths to make me feel welcome, as they garlanded me, arranged special church services for me to speak at, and fed me like a Maharaja. However, this Tamil pastor was also the eldest surviving male offspring on either side of the family. Suddenly in the midst of this eventful weekend, he had

---

[25] Hall, *The Hidden Dimension*, 1966, pp. 144–161.

to almost abandon me because of his duties connected with his mother's funeral and burial. In spite of the fact that he had one other brother there in the village with him that weekend, a brother who was not busy with the church work, my friend had no choice in the matter. In the pragmatic West, the two brothers would have compared notes, and if the siblings got along, the less-busy one would have volunteered to take the pressure off the brother tied up with other matters. Understanding differences in ordering, interculturally, will relieve some tensions we find in multicultural and cross-cultural situations.

Selection is another aspect of *organisation* and relates to 'whether there is something bound to something else by custom when any number of other items could "logically" serve the same purpose.'[26] In India, tea, curry, eggs, jam, chapatis, and bread make up a typical selection list for breakfasts, although not all will be eaten in the same breakfast. On the other hand, in part of the United States grits would be added to a standard list of edibles of orange juice, coffee, milk, cereal, toast, jam, bacon, ham, sausage, and eggs, whereas in another part of the country, grits would be unknown. Similarly, pan-fried potatoes would be commonplace as breakfast food in some places, but only as dinner fare in others. The same thing could be said about steak and potatoes. To serve jam and toast with any meal other than breakfast in India would be considered 'foreign'. You don't mix and match. There is a certain pattern of selection which is acceptable which differs across cultures.

To use a personal example of the intercultural dynamics surrounding this one issue, I find that international OM conferences held in Germany are an unpleasant experience as far as breakfast is concerned because conferees are served cold cuts (like sliced ham) for breakfast (which for me are luncheon meats), but the Germans don't give it a second thought. They've eaten that way for generations. The only place in OM where I have observed that a concerted effort is made to cater for the taste buds and eating habits of a diverse, international group is on the OM ships. Back on land, though, if half the world eats rice at every meal, why do we have to have mashed

---

bid., p. 158.

potatoes, even when people at an international gathering are guests in a country where mashed potatoes reign supreme? A little food for thought on globalisation!

Congruence is a third component of *organisation* where some helpful intercultural observations can be made that have a bearing on how international mission agencies can function more globally. Congruence has to do with a pattern of patterns, unlike selection and order, which have to do with the patterning of sets.[27] What might seem congruous in one culture, as in the way one is dressed, might be incongruous in another. To cite an example: in north India, in winter Indian gentlemen going to church often wear a suit with a tie and then a scarf around their necks and leather gloves on their hands, but no overcoat. To a Canadian, such attire is incongruous; we consider indoor winter attire is being mixed up with outdoor winter attire. Each has its place. But don't mix up the two.

Jokes in many cultures are often based on incongruities whereby someone is made fun of. In an intercultural mission group, it is wise to refrain from joking which points to the incongruities of one culture from the perspective of another. There is really nothing wrong with an Indian wearing a scarf directly on top of a suit! Furthermore, subtleties of such joking can be missed or misunderstood by one or more of the parties in the exchange, thus causing embarrassment at best, insult at worst. Such intercultural sensitivity is one sign that globalisation has taken root.

5. *Work.* Some cultures, as we have seen earlier, are substantially work-oriented whereas others are relation-oriented.[28] The former focus on tasks and principles of operation; the latter focus on relationships and how the operations of the task affect people. Therefore, the task-oriented Swiss society will find satisfaction in the achievement of work-related goals and might consider social activities to be a drain on productive use of time. In contrast, the people-oriented Argentinean culture

---

[27] *Ibid.,* p. 159.
[28] Adler, *International Dimensions,* 1991, pp. 27–28; Lingenfelter and Maye *Ministering Cross-Culturally,* pp. 82–94.

may find fulfilment in social interaction in the work place and sacrifice personal achievement in order to fit into the group. Often, such distinctions have been reduced to differences between personality types (such as when we distinguish between Type A and Type B personalities) but we are at a disadvantage in a multicultural organisation if we don't see that such differences can also be a result of culture. Ironically, Western World-based companies are now seeing the value of team work in furthering corporate goals and so are trying to de-programme employees who have been conditioned since birth to 'look out for number one', that is, to be individualistic and self-sufficient.[29]

How does this distinction work out in practice? Well, for Koreans, for example, personal feelings in a work setting tend to be more important than practical things. So when task-oriented Americans run rough-shod over other people's feelings on a missionary team, for the sake of getting the job done, they have initiated a serious communication problem with the Koreans on the team.

An example of the way people from distinct cultures approach work differently is that people-oriented people tend to dislike paperwork. For them conducting business face-to-face is definitely preferable to the Westernised practice of sending memos and copying to everyone under the sun![30] One person's efficient way of doing business becomes the next person's epitome of wasted time. Let us be careful that we do not create organisations after our own image; ones in which increasingly a large segment of the membership base feels out of place. If as much trouble was put into caring for members' needs and treating their cultures with respect as was put into meeting the needs of our target audience and understanding their culture, there wouldn't be such a high turnover of personnel in missions. A major cause of attrition in missions is an inability of missionaries to get along with their missionary colleagues.

---

on R. Katzenbach and Douglas K. Smith, *The Wisdom of Teams: Creating the Performance Organization* (New York: HarperCollins, 1994).
kdheo in Taylor, *Internationalising Training*, 1994, p. 58.

6. *Self-Worth.* Personal identity in some cultures is determined on the basis of merit, while in other cultures it is determined by birth and social rank.[31] We have already briefly touched on one aspect of this. *Status-focus* cultures result in the respect that one receives being fixed, with the individual involved being expected to play his or her prescribed role in the group.[32] People in Hindu cultures, for instance, are meant to associate primarily with those from their own caste. Society is regimented by a clearly-defined and complex caste system. In contrast, people from *achievement-focus* cultures grant and receive prestige on the basis of accomplishments. Hence, people socialise with those of relatively similar achievements, regardless of background. Engineers tend to mix with engineers. Lawyers with lawyers. Construction workers with other blue-collar workers. It would be erroneous to assume that just because an organisation is Christian, such differences in status across cultures do not affect the dynamics within the intercultural context.

An illustration of the role sensitivity training can have in facilitating globalisation comes from an incident observed where the training obviously had been lacking. At the OM conference, NETWORK '94, held in Falmouth, England in late April, 1994, board members, OM leaders, and key donors came from all over the world to consider OM's strategic plan up to the year AD 2000. During one of the seminars for board members, a Western OM leader reviewed the new purpose statement of the organisation. One of the goals of this seminar, as advertised, was to solicit input from the various boards so that they felt they were making a viable contribution to the changes in OM. However, rather than inviting discussion first, and then seeking some sort of consensus, the speaker made glowing and complimentary remarks about the purpose statement and then invited those present, who were in favour of the statement, to show their support by standing. Of course, everyone in the room stood. What the speaker failed to realise was that board members from such places as the Philippines, Hong Kong, Uruguay, India, Korea, and Singapore, whos

---

[31] Lingenfelter and Mayers, *Ministering Cross-Culturally*, pp. 95–104.
[32] Hofstede in Adler, *Dimensions*, 1991, pp. 46–50.

nationalities were all represented in this group, would not feel free to display any disagreement after such an introduction by the speaker. While the speaker may have been genuine in his enthusiasm and desire to elicit sincere feedback, he, in effect, had stage-managed the response. He had sent signals to those from high-context societies and those impressed by social rank that only one type of response would be deemed appropriate under the circumstances – affirmation of the proposed purpose statement as it was. Furthermore, those board members present who were from cultures where shame is a big issue, who were not adequately internationalised (a very real possibility under the circumstances), and who might have some reservations about the new direction in which OM was heading must have experienced a sense of frustration because they wouldn't have felt free to voice any disagreement. They didn't want to embarrass the leader of the seminar publicly by disagreeing with him in any way.

In numerous ways, mostly unconscious, Westerners in multinational missionary societies have been guilty of cultural imperialism. Our leaders do right in asking us to let love cover the multitude of such intercultural sins. However, we need to be careful not to spiritualise our failure to do our homework in overcoming ethnocentricism in intercultural settings. To the degree that we fail to find middle ground between diverse cultures, as we work side by side for the sake of the Gospel, we fail to globalise. The sort of learning environment that Senge and Schein preach as being essential to survival for tomorrow's corporations is what we must aim for in global partnerships in missions.[33]

The Role of Language

We should not underestimate the role that language plays in intercultural contexts.[34] When you have an international team functioning, such as is exhibited on the two OM ocean-going

---

Senge, *The Fifth*, pp. 302–305; Schein, *Organizational Culture*, pp. 363–373.
Hall, *Beyond Culture*, 1976, p. 117.

missionary ships, *Doulos* and *Logos II*, where you have forty
nationalities on board each ship from six different continents,
English is normally the language of team communication. That
is true whether you are talking about one of the ships as a whole
(macro-team level) or a ministry function on the ship, such as
the group running the book exhibition on the foredeck of the
ship (micro-team level). Whatever the case may be, the fact that
the majority of those on board do not have English as their
mother tongue puts the majority at a disadvantage. OM usually
allows only one language to be spoken as the 'team language',
that is, for intra-team communication. So, two Brazilians on an
international team cannot speak Portuguese to each other
unless it is done in private, out of the earshot of any other team
member. This problem is compounded if the culture the non-
English speakers come from is non-confrontational. English
grammar encourages directiveness, as is seen in the heavy
use of the active voice for verbs. If the active voice reduces
ambiguity because it designates, specifies, and seeks accuracy
(important qualities for scientific communication, it might be
added), imagine the struggle to fit in for the non-English
speaker, who faces the double challenge of a different language
and culture. In his or her language, such direct speech is
considered rude, untrustworthy, and embarrassing.[35]

Two-Thirds World people tend to be masters at indirect
speech. Therefore they are at a disadvantage when forced to
communicate in an unfamiliar language which is foreign to the
concepts and values of their own culture. Conversely, what
Elmer says is true: 'Westerners are not as skilled at reading
between the lines and interpreting people who express
themselves indirectly.'[36]

In connection with this issue, being a leader or transferring
potentiality of leadership to actual leadership is a problem
when the language of the leader is different from the language
of the team members. Andrew Pettigrew notes that language is
one of the key tools of leadership: 'A leader's effectiveness
is likely to be influenced by the language overlap with his fo‾

---

[35] Elmer, *Conflict*, pp. 47–52.
[36] *Ibid.*, p. 179.

lowers and by the extent to which a leader can create words that explain and thereby give order to collective experiences.[137]

In the past, this dynamic in how missionary colleagues functioned together may not have been highly relevant to realising effective ministry because most international missions were basically Anglo-American in makeup, but those days are changing as Two-Thirds Worlders enter the missionary workforce in increasing numbers, and not always through their own organisations. Little wonder then that those who train Asian missionaries complain that when Asian missionaries join international mission agencies, they have to learn two cultures and two languages: that of the Westernised mission agency and English – the white man's language.[38] In the same vein, the Asian missionary's success is judged partially by how well he or she adjusts to Westerners in the mission agency, whereas the Western missionary is judged by how well he or she adjusts to the local culture only.

Even the type of English spoken in an international mission agency results in discrimination which is covert. Although English is the medium for storing 80 per cent of the information found around the world in computers, the international airlines industry, and diplomacy, it is the native tongue for only twelve nations. Modified English speech is particularly prevalent in former British colonies, such as Singapore, India, and Nigeria, especially when English is not the mother tongue of their inhabitants. Examples of the metamorphosis of the British standard of English can be somewhat amusing, depending on your country of origin. Plural noun changes are common in India, such as, 'The street is full of litters.' Or hybrid words are frequently used in Singapore: 'shophouse' for store or shop, and 'towkay' for proprietor. In Nigeria it is perfectly acceptable to drop prepositions and nouns.[39] So when you are looking for an international standard for in-house mission communication,

Pettigrew, *ASQ*, p. 578.

Titus Loong in Taylor, *Training*, 1991, p. 44; Y. J. Cho and David H. Greenlee, 'tinational Teams in International Missions.

thony Flint, 'Your English, My English, or Our English?' *The Toronto Star* ry 23, 1994), p. E8.

which English standard should be chosen? The fact of the matter is that language norms in the English-speaking world have to do with national identity and pride, so is it possible for a win-win situation to actually exist here in an international mission? At least let's acknowledge that it is a problem.

Realistically, multicultural organisations can function effectively and efficiently only if they possess a common language.[40] Usually this will be English, since it is the most widespread language on the globe. However, because of the value and culture-laden nature of language, it might be wise for large international mission organisations, like YWAM or SIM, to develop the following strategy in order to alleviate the pressures faced by their Two-Thirds World constituencies in becoming global partners in a common enterprise:

1. Not require non-English speakers to learn English as an entry point to the organisation if the host country they will work in speaks another language. For example, an evangelism team working in France composed of Koreans, Germans, and French missionaries could use French as the team medium, rather than English.

2. Allow for opportunity to communicate publicly in languages other than English in international gatherings of the mission membership. Of course, in this sort of situation a translation team would have to be on hand. Simultaneous translation into main languages of participants should also be intentionalised.

3. Require missionaries, who are career workers, to learn another language as part of their lifelong learning commitment. A phenomenon of modern missions is the large number of specialists who work in home office or headquarters settings and never have to learn another language. Their work is strictly in-house. A computer programmer working in a mission headquarters in Worthing, England who hails from Ireland does no have to enter the typical missionary experience learning a foreign language (well, maybe apart fr overcoming a foreign accent!). However, this rea

---

[40] Ohmae, *World*, 1990, p. 94.

breeds ethnocentricism in large organisations which can afford such degrees of specialisation. Interestingly enough, aware of this very problem, St. John's Seminary in California has a requirement that students learn another language before they can be ordained. This high standard has been put in place because of this seminary's prioritising of globalisation.[41]

It is well worth observing here that Europeans are often less ethnocentric as missionaries than their North American counterparts. Is it coincidental that Europeans study several languages in school, with many being at least bilingual, whereas North Americans may go through school without ever having been exposed for more than a year or two to the systematic learning of another language?

Let me add a note of humour to this subject of how to communicate interculturally with this by-line taken from an issue of OM's in-house journal, *Relay*:

Having spoken English as the preferred language in the EEC, the European Parliament has commissioned a feasibility study in ways of improving efficiency in communications between Government departments.

European officials have often pointed out that English spelling is unnecessarily difficult. For example, *cough, plough, through,* and *thorough*. What is clearly needed is a phased programme of changes to iron out these anomalies. The programme would, of course, be administered by a committee of staff at top level by participating nations.

In the first year, for example, the committee would suggest using 's' in instead of the soft 'c'. Sertainly, sivil servants in all sities would reseive this news with joy. Then the hard 'c' could be replaced by 'k' sinse both letters are pronounced alike. Not only would this klear up konfusion in the minds of klerikal workers, but typewriters kould be made with one less letter.

There would be growing enthusiasm when in the

---

[41] Ronald C. White, 'Globalization is Closing in on Us,' *Theological Education* ?7(2) (Spring, 1991): 51–57.

sekond year, it kould be announsed that the troublesome
'ph' would henseforth be written 'f'. This would make
words like 'fotograf' twenty per sent shorther in print.

In the third year, publik akseptanse of the new spelling
kan be expekted to reash the stage where more
komplikated shanges are possible. Government would
enkourage the removal of double letters which have
always been a deterent to akurate speling.

Much more needs to be stated on the subject of how international mission agencies can be transformed from the inside out
in order to demonstrate that they have moved beyond internationalisation to globalisation. To evaluate globalisation of an
organisation only in terms of external factors without considering the internal culture is to look only skin deep. Or, as *Apollo 7*
astronaut Walter M. 'Wally' Schirra Jr. observed from space
when looking back at earth, you couldn't see the distinguishing
features of the geography of the world's nations; but they are
there! Similarly, no matter how much impetus there is to blur
the significance of nationhood and culture, their reality must be
understood and respectfully allowed for as we create a new
synergy made up of parts larger than any one culture or nation
in the cause of world evangelisation. That requires getting very
practical! The next chapter reflects on even more areas where,
for globalisation of missions to occur, the inner world of organisations needs to change.

NINE

Let's Get Practical!

Conflict between missionary colleagues does not always come out into the open. I'll never forget leaving India for the first time, after three and a half years there. I was standing on the flat rooftop of our missions' base in New Delhi, ready to fly out to Brussels the next day. I was talking with an Indian brother who had worked closely with me for the previous two years. I was taken aback when suddenly he blurted out, 'David, if you can't learn to be more gentle in your dealings with us Indians, don't bother coming back.' I was shocked. I had always thought that he and I had a good relationship. We have since become genuinely good friends, but I learned a couple of things through that incident: I needed to change something about my character, and I needed to become a better student of Indian culture.

You see, globalisation of missions does not occur simply by virtue of the fact that Indians and British work together for the evangelisation of the final frontiers, but only when they have learned to work together as equal partners. For that to happen, international organisations must get practical. In this chapter we will explore several more ways that missions can make specific internal changes so as to facilitate this globalisation. Young adults looking for the right international mission to join should look more at these qualities than at how glossy and contemporary the recruiting brochures are.

Handling Intercultural Conflict

If secular management literature is accurate, as we saw earlier, international missions face conflict more at the micro as opposed to the macro level. International leaders (executives) tend to handle intercultural ambiguity and communication better, and identify more positively to pan-organisational as opposed to parochial perspectives, than do their co-workers in the trenches. This is an observation personally validated during the years I have worked with OM. On localised international teams it has been my experience that friction between team members, who hail from very different parts of the world can be quite pronounced, even though it may only exist as an undercurrent of tension most of the time. However in top-leadership levels I have noticed more of a fraternity in operation. Racially-related sniping seems to kept to a minimum. Personality clashes and tensions over intercultural values are dealt with graciously and nipped in the bud.

In the questionnaire conducted among OM leaders, referred to in the chapter on leadership styles, some practical suggestions on how to alleviate intercultural conflict were made. One Oriental respondent to the questionnaire said, 'I would change the process of [international leaders' meetings]. Instead of open expression of individual opinion, it should be done on a regional basis first and feedback [could come] this way. This provides a restraint on first-language English speakers and cultures where group opinion comes before individual.' In his survey of 160,000 managers and employees in sixty countries, Dutch researcher, Geert Hofstede, observed three of four areas where differences in work-related values and attitudes could be traced to culture: individualism/collectivism, power distance, and uncertainty avoidance (masculinity/femininity was the other factor).[1] Most Occidental cultures are individualistic, where people define themselves as individuals. Collectivists, usually from Oriental cultures, define themselves by tight social frameworks in which people distinguish between their group and other groups. However, within the organisation of

---

[1] Cited in Adler, *International Dimensions*, 1983, p. 46ff.

most missions conflict resolution occurs in ways that favour individualist cultures, not collectivist ones.

More intensive dialoguing needs to occur between Western World and Two-Thirds World leaders so as to develop styles of international decision making and management that are more user-friendly for non-Westerners. One appropriate innovation would be to agree to make wider use of mediators to resolve certain kinds of conflict. Sergei Frank, global lawyer and marketing executive, stresses the importance of negotiating in international business contexts, maintaining that one can do so from a position of strength if one is sensitive to the competitor's culture.[2] Elmer and other cultural anthropologists similarly urge that such intercultural conflict-resolution be handled by neutral mediators respected by both sides.[3] The engagement of this sort of middleman enables Two-Thirds World parties trapped in conflict to avoid face-to-face confrontation, thereby minimising the potential loss of face, or dishonour, so often part of the outcome of relational stress management.

While people from some Two-Thirds World cultures may be able to handle interpersonal conflict between equal-status leaders decisively, because of a hierarchical view of authority, the same people can be paralysed when the conflict is between those at different levels of leadership. Then, 'Might makes right!' Commenting on the Asian perspective on leadership status, Maureen Ma says,

> As Asian society is often conceived as having different levels of authority or rank, an attitude of respect and loyalty towards the leader or the person in charge is expected and given . . . . As the personhood of a leader is closely identified with his position, challenging a leader's ways of doing things, may be taken as an attack on the personal integrity of the leader. When heated issues are being discussed, a great deal of skill and tact would come into play to avoid causing offence to the person concerned. An Asian wouldn't like to see his leader being criticised in

Sergei Frank, 'Negotiating – An Underestimated Skill', *Silver Kris* (December, '3): 34–38.
 mer, *Conflict*, pp. 65–79.

public. This is in marked contrast to the western view of leadership which allows for the leader's proposals or projects to be criticised or challenged without it being seen as a personal attack on the leader himself.[4]

While there is some deference to power and status among Westerners, inherent individualism and democratic values enable Westerners to be more comfortable in seeking to resolve any sort of dispute, regardless of who is involved and what their respective leadership status is. Given these different outlooks, a mediator levels the playing field for all participants in intercultural conflict.

Peter Senge, in *The Fifth Discipline*, similarly explicates the effectiveness of mediation through what he calls 'advocacy and inquiry'.[5] The essence of this style of conflict resolution is to set a goal of not winning the argument but of finding the right solution. This approach balances one's point of view with the opponent's. Sometimes, this blending of advocacy with inquiry is only achievable through an appointed mediator. Stephen Covey, in *Principled-Centred Leadership*, propounds a theory bearing resemblance to Senge's in calling for 'win-win' attitudes to conflict resolution. Crucial to its success is developing the mindset of 'seeking first to understand, then to be understood' – one of his seven habits of highly-effective people. He eloquently observes:

> Does it take courage to *not* be understood first? Think about it. Think about the problems you face. You tend to think, 'You need to understand me, but you don't understand. I understand you, but you don't understand me. So let me tell you my story first, and then you can say what you want.' And the other person says, 'Okay, I'll try to understand.' But the whole time they're 'listening', they're preparing their reply. They're just pretending to listen, selectively listening. . . . The other person is tuned out unless he feels understood.[6]

---

[4] Maureen Ma, 'What Do Asians Expect From Their Leaders?', paper presented to OM Euroleaders' Meetings of November, 1993.
[5] Senge, *The Fifth Discipline*, pp. 198–202.
[6] Covey, p.45.

Compromise is frowned on in many Western cultures. Forth-rightness is considered to be an admirable quality in a leader. Look at how far bluntness took Winston Churchill and the Allied cause in World War II. The British fondly say about a Yorkshireman, 'You can tell someone from Yorkshire, but you can't tell him much.' In North America, compromise is considered a weakness, as seen in the disparaging comment, 'Oh, he's acting like a politician'. Accuracy and precision are often associated with truthfulness. Confession of fault is deemed to be a sign of strength of character. Biblical justification is ferreted out for all these virtues. However, all too often Two-Thirds World societies have diametrically-opposed standards.

Matthew 18:15–17 is almost always proffered as the proof-text for defending a more confrontational method of resolving interpersonal tensions, whether in local churches or international mission societies. Only a cursory study of Scripture, however, leads one to the conclusion that there is more than just one way to handle relational problems in the Body of Christ. 'Love covers a multitude of sins'. . . . 'As much as lies within you be at peace with all men'. . . . 'Bear with one another and forgive whatever grievances you may have against one another'. . . . 'A soft answer turns away wrath.' To quote just a few.

Jesus is an excellent model of the alternative approach. He did not always confront sin by throwing people out of temples, as we see in John 8:1–11. He did not blow out a smouldering wick or bruise a fragile reed in the way he dealt with vulnerable people (Mt. 12:20). Accusations by Pharisees were often met with silence or deflected by a question, in spite of his sometime biting criticism of these religious leaders. To teach the disciples that they should not vie for prominence in service for him, Jesus beckoned a child to receive blessing from him (Mk.9:33–37). In such situations, failing to answer the charge or question directly was not avoidance, but a demonstration of patience, waiting for a better time to resolve the problem. This is a method frequently advocated in Scripture (e.g., Prov. 15:1; Jas.

his book *Cross-Cultural Conflict*, Elmer shows how the of the Hebrew midwives protecting the life of Moses

(Exodus 1) demonstrates that managing a conflict through indirect methods is not necessarily deceptive or deceitful.[7] The
midwives were silent in response to the Pharaoh's command,
and deflected blame when confronted about allowing Hebrew
male babies to live. The text concludes: 'God was kind to the
midwives.' Would he have been kind if he was angry at their
alleged disobedience? Another example of using an indirect
method to handle conflict was Esther's sense of timing in
revealing the plight of her people to the Persian king.

Obviously, there are nuances in handling this dilemma that
are not readily apparent, perhaps most of all to a Westerner.
Meanwhile, Two-Thirds Worlders read these Biblical stories
and smile. They know what it means to use silence, inaction, or
a third-party mediator to resolve their interpersonal problems.
Rather than the Westerner assuming that such a strategy is
unethical, there needs to be an openness to using this phleg-
matic approach, on the basis that the Bible does not condemn
such behaviour and that all cultures are imperfect in their ability to objectively screen out cultural bias through the sieve of
Scripture.

Strategic placement of gifted Two-Thirds World nationals

Suspicion between former colonies in the Two-Thirds World
and their Western World colonisers has not entirely ended.
Hence, when global organisations exist which throw many different nationalities together, they need to take practical steps to
ensure that organisation-wide decisions are perceived as being
non-paternalistic and non-imperialistic. It is not enough to build
solid friendships across the cultural divide, as was intimated
earlier in the book, but structural realities are crucial in being a
harbinger of globalisation. One such case is in the selecting of
Two-Thirds World nationals for key international posts within
the organisation. These nationals need to be respected as leaders
in their own national spheres of service and influence first, but
then also increasingly, at the international, or organisation-wide
level.

---

[7] Elmer, *Conflict*, p.130.

Who is the International Director of the organisation? Who is the Chief Financial Officer? Who handles major personnel decisions? In most of these positions key roles have historically been filled by Westerners in typical interdenominational mission organisations. That must change if we are to truly speak the language of globalisation.

In OM, the trend has been slowly changing to include more Two-Thirds World nationals at the top-leadership levels. For example, in 1994, of fifty-two official or newly-opened fields in OM, thirty-five were led by nationals.[8] It is not uncommon among international mission organisations, though, to discover veteran expatriate missionaries still in the leadership roles of their field, decades after the work in that field has begun. One might argue that to be globalised authentically we should not worry about the nationality of the leader, instead we should put the best person into the job. Theoretically, that may be true, but until Two-Thirds World people have made more inroads into the corridors of power in missions we will have to 'discriminate'.

Incidentally, in the OM of 1994, there was not one case of an OM field leader, who was not a national of the country he was working in, being from somewhere else in the Two-Thirds World. Without seeing parity as a panacea for fashioning globalisation within missions' cultures, it is the view propounded here that, for the time being at least, globalisation must be viewed in terms of favouring Two-Thirds World interests!

The top leadership level in OM is called the Executive Committee. It is made up of the co-ordinators of each of the regions of the OM world, of which there are over ten, plus the International Director, and the Associate International Director. There may be a number of 'fields' within each 'area'. Slightly more than 50 per cent of the areas are led by nationals, that is, by

---

The term *field* as used by OM is defined in its *Policy Manual* as 'the main unit which ministry is based and may vary greatly in size. It is the main operaal/leadership/management unit. It is also the unit to which personnel ally belong and by which they are administered and cared for. Frequently and a country may coincide but a *field* may cover more than a country. also may be more than one *field* in a country.'

those who hail from one of the countries ('fields') in the area. Thus, Rodney Hui, from Singapore, is the area leader for East Asia. Joseph D'Souza represents India. Tony Kirk of England represents Western Europe. However, in not one instance where a non-national represents an area, is that area co-ordinator from the Two-Thirds World. Whether unconsciously or not, missions must come to grips with their predilection to favour those from the West for executive missionary roles.

Again referring to OM's track record (by no means a poor one in relation to many of its counterparts on the global mission scene) neither of its two premier positions at the time of writing is filled by a non-Westerner. George Verwer, an American, (long-time resident of Great Britain) is the International Director. Peter Maiden, an English man, is the Associate International Director. All key international posts in personnel, finance, and information services are filled by Westerners.

Aware of the anomaly between its stated goal of globalisation and the filling of top leadership roles by Westerners, OM has specifically indicated its intention of seeing fields increasingly led by nationals and area co-ordinators indigenous to the region of the OM world they represent. Positively augmenting this strategy would be OM's selecting of suitably-qualified Two-Thirds World nationals, of whom there are some, for pivotal international roles and posts. Currently, Chinese, Indians, and Koreans particularly show promise of being ready to assume these sorts of positions within OM. Two-Thirds World fields must also be prepared to act selflessly for this to happen. They can't keep all their best people for themselves. It may require redeployment of key people from their front-line work in order for globalisation to be facilitated. Servanthood cuts both ways.

The matter of spiritual gifting and gender will be an issue too for progressive-thinking missions in the next decade. Powers that be, nonetheless, must be careful of the bias that says tha' because 'they do it differently', therefore 'they don't do it right Spiritual gifting does not come in certain skin colours or certa accents (1 Cor. 12:11). International mission agencies v always be enriched by empowering those who come f non-traditional leadership sources.

Working Towards Flatter Structures

Does globalisation render centralised structures superfluous or all the more necessary? Although the technological breakthroughs impacting the contemporary global company may not always apply to the global mission agency, the consensus on the world scene is that the age of information and technology is engendering the dismantling of highly-centralised organisations.[9] With easy access to information and communication, work can be done in small groups which are isolated geographically. Flat rather than top-down management is the order of the day. Peter Drucker is right when he calls such knowledge workers 'executives', because they are expected to act on their knowledge to make decisions, plan, organise, integrate, motivate, and measure, just as the president of the company might be expected to do in larger areas.[10] Previously, in the industrial age, that knowledge was held in the hands of a few people: the managers and executives, with the average person contributing to the company's welfare through manual labour. Now a shoe company may need to employ as many people in computerised designing and marketing as it does in hand stitching leather. These changes require individualised expertise, not based on manual skills, but on knowledge skills.

A side effect of 'flatter' companies is the proliferation of greater diversity and the creation of an expectation of it – both in companies and in the larger culture. Let me give you an example of what I am talking about. These days when I fly internationally I can expect an increasing amount of choice in the inflight entertainment offered. On Lufthansa, on a recent flight to India, I could watch the latest newscast in English or German, watch some cartoons, observe computerised information about progress of the flight, see a movie, and then listen to a variety of audio programmes, ranging from classical music to opera, ballads, smooth jazz, soft rock, easy listening, country, Arabic, Hindi, Latin, Korean, Japanese, Chinese, German folk

---

for example, see Deal and Kennedy, *Corporate Culture*, p. 177; Ohmae, *The derless World*, 1990, pp. 87, 100.

ter Drucker, *The Effective Executive* (New York: HarperCollins, 1996), 26–533.

music, golden oldies, comedy, or I could follow a children's programme, a teen magazine programme, or an English language course. In other words, at the same time as there is standardisation of what is offered, there is enhancement of it and a demand for diversity.

Computer technology is having a profound impact on the way missions communicate in-house and to their constituency, such as by e-mail and by people-friendly direct mail. In the last week I have received e-mail from around the OM world from places like Central Asia, England, India, the United States, and Canada. Be that as it may, this technology does not promise to give an edge in cross-cultural church planting, nor in keeping a short-term missionary on the field for a lifetime of service. Yet the expectations of a younger generation reared on the flat line, highly participative organisational structure has implications for the future of doing missions. So does the infusion of multi-nationality missionary forces on what has traditionally been the privy of Anglo-Americans. Globe-spanning missions will by virtue of necessity provide structures that meet the expectations of two interest groups: Generation X Westerners and emerging non-Western missionaries. Individual fields will need to be furnished with a fair degree of autonomy. Koreans will not want head office in Edinburgh telling them how to establish a pension plan for their missionaries. National missionaries in Bangladesh will not want to be told how to erect their churches by the international office in Atlanta. Diversity will reign supreme.

International functions of mission organisations will need to concentrate on providing services rather than increasing their span of control. Services such as pastoral care, fund-raising, missiological research, and teaching/preaching ministry are well appreciated across cultures and when done on an ad hoc basis, as opposed to being systematised centrally, do not pose a threat to local autonomy. Centralised structures also serve to socialise the outlying areas to the corporate purpose statement vision, values, ethos, and goals. In a word, central structure preserve the *culture* of the entire entity. This promotion the corporate culture is achieved through things like visit individual fields by international leaders, organising

national, regional, and international conferences for the personnel of the mission, personal mentoring of potential leaders
by overall leaders, memos, and deepening of a vast network of
interpersonal relationships.

In one sense, becoming globalised should result in a mission
demonstrating greater diversity at the local level because its
leaders and personnel there are respected and trusted enough
not to be micro-managed from abroad. An example of what is
being talked about here comes from Japan. Through the
developing of the Sony company, Akio Morita fashioned an
entertainment electronics giant that is truly global in scope.
Started in Japan, Sony is synonymous with such consumer
items as the Walkman and computer products like the 3.5 inch
floppy disk. Sony's global success is partially due to Morita's
insistence that its products appeal to local tastes. Factories have
mushroomed in places like Bangkok, Wales, and Tijuana.
Sony's growth strategy for the nineties revolved around this
globalisation. Morita calls their concept 'global localisation', by
which he means decentralising authority, adapting product
lines, working conditions, and marketing ploys to the local
situation, all within the focus of a coherent international
strategy.[11]

Such 'global localisation' will combine the free flow of
resources internationally with the preservation of local fla-
vour. Missionaries can be deployed in and out of the
unreached world from any part of the mission world. Expertise, money, and ministry concentration which require some
sort of international (centralised) orchestration will know no
national boundaries. But local and regional distinctives will be
preserved and esteemed. For instance, some countries will
require a highly-indigenised approach to things like church
planting. Americans will be less welcome in India than Canadians. British missionaries should probably not be part of an
international ministry team targeting Argentina. Latins fit in
extremely well in Morocco and are to be preferred to other
nationalities in a multinational pool of prospective workers

ichard J. Barnet and John Cavanagh, *Global Dreams: Imperial Corporations*
e New World Order (New York: Simon & Shuster, 1994), pp. 63–67.

who are serious about evangelising this North African Muslim country. A complex global partnership allows for positive synergy in ministry, without standardisation of ministry by top-down management, which chokes off legitimate contextualisation.

A collegial-participative structuring of the organisation, not an authoritarian-paternalistic one, will encourage the Two-Thirds World's shaping of the agenda of the organisation into the twenty-first century. Flatter structures also free Two-Thirds World missionaries to relate more easily to home churches. This home church link is more of a felt need with some non-Western missionaries than many may realise. According to Joshua Ogawa of Japan, 'Asian [missionaries] are often regarded as representatives of their home churches in Asia. This understanding may be true with the Western counterparts, but it is more so with the Asians because of the corporate nature of their society. Most Asian members are pioneer missionaries with many expectations from their churches at home.'[12] Globalisation means responding to such expectations sensitively.

Will mission organisations survive such seemingly conflicting goals? Can unity and diversity coexist, realistically? In chapters two and three, a theological construct was advanced which claimed it was possible. In all fairness, it has to be stated that the jury is still out on this matter. A further generation of missionaries will have to come and go before any meaningful assessment can be made. According to secular management experts like Deal and Kennedy, this sort of globalisation will work just because such corporations 'tolerate and encompass differences.'[13] However, diversity at the local level will flourish in an international company or mission only if leaders continue to be bearers and promoters of the global corporate culture.

Having made these comments about the value of flatter structure lines in global missions, it should be remarked that

---

[12] Joshua Ogawa, 'The Benefits and Problems of Internationalizing Missions in Taylor, *Training*, 1994, p. 174.
[13] Deal and Kennedy, *Corporate Culture*, p. 153; cf. Schein, *Organizational C ture*, p. 370.

this kind of organisational pattern may not always be advisable in certain national (field) situations. Hofstede has done a landmark study referred to earlier in which he distinguishes variables of behaviour among companies of many nationalities. One of these, we saw, was power distance. Countries vary, he found, in the degree to which people in a hierarchical set-up perceive greater or lesser ability to control each other's behaviour. People in high-power distance nations, such as Mexico or the Philippines, perceive more inequality between superiors and subordinates than do people in low-power distance nations like Austria or Denmark. Perhaps not coincidentally, in the DSI survey of OM leaders, mentioned in a previous chapter, the respondent with the second highest 'directive'-style score of the twenty-two nationalities in the sample was Indian.[14] In high-power distance societies, much deference is given to the overall leader, who functions as a father figure, even a kind of godfather.[15] Therefore, globalisation may mean flatter international structures and yet unchanged hierarchical local structures.

A practical way of diffusing the centralisation inherent in globalised entities is perhaps to welcome outside nationalities on to local boards. Cross pollination of this nature is particularly desirable from East to West. Sony of Japan is an example of how this works. It has an American and a Swiss on its board of directors. They are not at a disadvantage in board meetings because translators whisper in their ears at the Tokyo-based gatherings.[16] Luis Bush has raised this issue with regard to mission organisations, wondering how decisions, policies, and budgets can be determined at the partnership level when each organisation in the partnership is autonomous.[17] Exchanging board members is one way this mutual accountability can work in practice.

---

[4] Rowe and Mason, who developed the DSI, define the 'directive' style (to ̣iew) as the one characterised by its practical bent on the 'here and now'. ̣ple with this style prefer structure, are action-oriented, decisive, and ̣t-oriented. They tend to be authoritarian and function best in a hierarchical ̣isational structure where they can exercise more control.

̣r, *Dimensions*, 1991, pp. 27–54.

̣t and Cavanagh, *Dreams*, p. 66.

̣*Funding*, 1990, pp. 51–52.

Sharing of Technical and Educational Expertise

A detailed defence of both financial partnership in the globalisation of missions and the sharing of human resources for front-line or leadership ministry has already been made. More needs to be said about the this latter aspect of sharing. Numerous mission agencies already tap computer expertise from wherever it can be found, generally from Western sources. Development of customised software is commonplace among larger organisations. But there are other areas of giftedness and skills that should not be ignored. Loaning or redeploying accountants, Bible teachers, church-planting experts, and evangelists would make for a more effective utilisation of resources in global missions.

This flow of people resources does not need to be all one way. To cite one example, non-Westerners often are excellent evangelists. Concerning placement of Westerners, Schipper dreams of bands of roving missiologists who take their expertise to Two-Thirds World sites where the national missionary force has not yet had the insights and know-how that Western agencies have gained from their decades of involvement in cross-cultural ministry.[18] Similarly, Pate argues that: 'Utilising modular training systems and international teams of experts [makes] possible that fully transferable training could be offered by qualified instructors. Through such innovative efforts, high quality missionary training from indigenous, experienced instructors could eventually be available to most missionary candidates around the world.'[19]

An unfolding model of this idea of sharing specialities is the starting of a non-residential graduate school by OM-India in a joint venture with Briercrest Biblical Seminary of Saskatchewan, Canada. The genius of this programme, which offers a Master of Arts in Leadership and Management, or in Missiology, which is accredited by Briercrest, is that it enable nationals in full-time ministry to study part-time without t

---

[18] G. Schipper, 'Non-Western Missionaries: Our Newset Challenge,' *Ev* *cal Missions Quarterly* 24(3) (July, 1988): 200.
[19] Pate in Taylor, *Internationalising*, 1991, p. 38.

much expense or hardship being imposed on their ministries and families. This sort of distance education programme may be commonplace in the West where there is a mania for continuous education (lifelong learning), but it is a foreign concept, for the most part, in a place like India. The programme is designed along the Doctor of Ministry lines, now popular in North America especially, which combines self-study with a practical theology emphasis in two weeks of residential classes held every six months for four-year cycles. Teachers from Briercrest, (of which I am one), donate their time to teach these courses and are blended in with Indian instructors. Required courses are taken in the basic theological disciplines of NT studies, OT studies, theology, and church history, but majors exist in leadership and missiology. Leadership development, in particular, is a noted Briercrest strength. Thus, students, all of whom have at least ten years experience in the ministry as a condition to being accepted into the programme, are simultaneously able to upgrade relevant ministry skills and gain a recognised degree. Other higher learning institutions are beginning to offer these kinds of educational opportunities to Two-Thirds World people, like the Oxford Centre for World Missions, but they usually require some sort of residency period as a condition to obtaining the degree. The Briercrest model has counterparts in Africa and also in Asia. It is attractive because it is cost effective, and accesses international money and expertise without totally sacrificing contextualised learning. Nevertheless it is far from being accessible to a wide range of up and coming Christian leaders in the Two-Thirds World.

Westerners who are sensitive to the history of paternalism and imperialism in modern missions need to accept the fact that Two-Thirds World mission leaders, as we have seen in some of their observations made earlier in the book, are still crying out for help in areas other than money. They do not have the lengthy track record of cross-cultural ministry that many Western-based mission agencies have, like the Church Missionary Society, and are asking for help in training national missionaries before expectations are built up too much. Along these lines, Jenssen makes a valid point when he observes:

Culturally, the many calls to 'Hurry up!' only motivate a minority of societies. If the burgeoning missions force of Africans, Asians, and Latin Americans is really needed to help fulfil the *Missio Dei*, then we need to quit trying to motivate them as if they were 'hurry up' cultures. Most of these brethren have a world-view that says there is plenty of time to do whatever is really important.[20]

An example of this measured response to a Two-Thirds World felt need for better preparation in gearing up for a massive contribution to the missionary cause, is seen in what the World Evangelical Fellowship Mission Commission is doing. The commission, according to William Taylor, works with some forty leaders and thirty movements in the Two-Thirds World to empower them through missionary training consultations, seminars, and publications.[21] Such partnerships invest Western specialised help wisely without overshadowing initiatives being taken by Two-Thirds World missionary movements.

The Value of International Teams

Those who have worked on international mission teams are fairly predictable in their reaction. They are believers in them! The commendation of international teams is not wholesale, however. International teams are reputed to bring added insight to the dynamics of cross-cultural ministry, and to allow for a richer mix of skills and gifting, but they also drain a lot of energy through intra-team resolving of conflict and the necessity for complex communication. From early on in OM's existence, one of its distinctives has been a commitment to engage in ministry cross-culturally through international teams. My first OM team was for the summer of 1971 in southern France. On that team we had people from France, Sweden, the United States, Great Britain, Germany, Switzerland, and Canada. My first team in India in 1972 had on it Indians,

---

[20] Robert Rasmussen, 'Global Push or Grandiose Schemes?' *EMQ*, 32(3) (1996): 276–277.
[21] William Taylor, 'Lessons of Partnership,' *EMQ*, (October, 1995): 406–

Briton, an American, and myself. Today, it would be likely that the team would include a Latin, a Korean, and more nationals of the country in which it is working.

In venues where Christianity is perceived as being a Western religion, like Pakistan, an international team models the universality of the faith for the locals. National Christians are able to see that it is possible to live together in harmony and unity.

However, the real beauty of the international team is that it broadens the prospects for effective ministry. Cho and Greenlee have identified this potential in their study of OM teams with which they were associated: 'Brazilian vibrancy, Korean discipline, and American organization can complement each other to make the combined unit much stronger than the individual parts.'[22]

On the other hand, we must be careful not to glamorise international teams. As previously mentioned, they can bring with them much energy-dissipating misunderstanding as a result of varying thought processes, ways of communicating (nonverbal and verbal) and languages spoken, among the diverse cultures represented on the team.[23] The danger of such teams is that rather than concentrating on contextualising to the host culture the team fusses with contextualising between team members!

Sensitivity to the right multinational blend on international teams cannot be stressed enough. Bush compares this putting together of the international team to assembling an orchestra.[24] Different instrumentalists are needed in varying quantities for each performance. Even a chuch-planting team in Mozambique may need to look different from the church-planting one forming in Spain. In regions where there is hostility to Christianity because of historical baggage, as in the Middle East due to the Crusades, certain nationalities will be tolerated less than others. Colonialism also puts a damper on some nationalities functioning effectively in specific parts of the

and Greenlee, 'Multinational Teams', p. 7.

'ra Mackin, 'Multinational Teams: Smooth as Silk or Rough as
?,' *EMQ* 28(2) (April, 1992): 134–140.

nd Lotz, *Partnering*, p. 89.

world. Hence, Japanese missionaries are not especially welcome in South Korea. Germans face an uphill battle for acceptance in France. Americans might as well forget about Libya. Two-Thirds World missionaries will probably be more 'placeable' in the Gospel-resistant 10–40 Window nations than their comrades coming from 'imperialistic' Western World backgrounds.

Furthering the successful deployment of effective international teams will be pre-field education. Before joining such a team, each team member should be led through self-analysis that forces him or her to come to grips with cultural specifics of his or her own culture. Orientation on intercultural differences can be provided, supplemented by a reading programme, using materials like Paul Hiebert's book, *Anthropological Insights for Missionaries*, or Sherwood Lingenfelter and Marvin Mayers' book, *Ministering Cross-Culturally: An Incarnational Model for Personal Relationships*.

In its efforts to globalise, OM established a Globalisation Committee in 1993 which was charged with the responsibility of proposing concrete ways OM could promote globalisation within its ranks. Maureen Ma, chair of this committee, did an admirable job in pulling together various ideas in order to submit a list of such proposals to the Executive Committee of OM. To deepen intercultural awareness, she called for topics on cultural anthropology, intercultural living, and cross-cultural ministry to be covered at all OM training conferences. Anyone joining OM, whether for a summer or a lifetime, can now expect to receive this teaching. The new OMer will be equipped to serve on a global team as never before.

Maureen provides an illustration of why this kind of orientation is needed and how it could lead to some positive changes in the way OM does things. Surely her advice would be relevant for many other missions. Speaking of OM's international business meetings, she says:

> In the West, often issues are presented with a rather pu
> sales pitch appealing more to the emotions. Somet'
> there is a confrontational attitude exhibited, making
> of opposing viewpoints in order to substantiate one

position. A culture that values relationships, not points of view, will find this approach abrasive.

Maureen is from Hong Kong and so speaks with some authority on the issue at hand.

Come what may, as missions become global-literate, they will increasingly find the positive spin-offs of international teams outweighing the negatives in most places where local exigencies prevent such teams from being fielded. Like it or not, in many of these settings, the crown jewels in the team will be brothers and sisters from the Two-Thirds World.

TEN

Are Contextualisation and Globalisation on a Collision Course?

One of the greatest church-planting movements of the twentieth century has taken place in India. It all began in the Winnipeg YMCA in the autumn of 1929 when Canadian, John Hayward, met Indian, Bakht Singh. Through John's hospitality this lonely, engineering Sikh student, far from home, came to believe in Christ. In 1933, having been discipled, Bakht Singh returned home to India where he founded one thousand churches over the course of his life-time. Brother Bakht Singh is still alive and well into his nineties at the time of writing. Many Indians consider him to be India's greatest living Christian.

Keen observers of the Indian church will undoubtedly maintain that one of the key reasons for the proliferation of the Bakht Singh Assemblies, as they are known, is their indigenous nature. Generally speaking, their congregations sit on the floor, men on one side of the room and women and children (except for older sons) on the other side. Adornment of the walls is sparse, usually with Scripture texts. Songs are sung with Indian instrumentation. Services are not time-regulated. The usual length of service is about three hours, which includes the breaking of bread, reflecting Brethren influences, as do some other practices. Leadership is shared through elders, great authority and respect being granted them. Services are often followed by a communal meal, served on banana leaf, while participants sit cross-legged on the floor eating with their right hands.

Why mention this here? Because, ironically, today the Bakht Singh Assemblies are also pointed to by some as an example of how *not* to contextualise the church in India. True, Bakht Singh worship may be an improvement, critics say, on the old British-style, one-hour, pew-and-pulpit based services which predominate in the mainline Protestant churches, but a Hindu or Muslim seeker or convert will still feel uncomfortable in the Bakht Singh Assemblies. No effort is made to avoid theological language new converts or seekers will be unfamiliar with, let alone use equivalents from Sanskrit. 'Separation' is a hot topic among Bakht Singh wallas and that includes separation from anything that resembles Hinduism. Spiritual separation is equated with being against virtually anything in the culture that is not specifically Christian, akin to the position taken by Western World fundamentalist churches. Culture, then, is seen as being essentially irredeemable.

Using India as a backdrop, we need to ponder one area of missiology where globalisation seems to be on a collision course with 'progress' – contextualisation. A great debate is currently occurring in India over the possibility of 'churchless Christianity' – a debate which epitomises the tension between globalisation and contextualisation, which is somewhat the same debate as that between Gospel and culture in any churched society.

In essence, the churchless Christianity thesis is that those who have brought the Gospel to India have so intruded their own cultural bias into the discipling process that the end product has been the shaping of a strange creature, one that is a misfit to true Indian culture. Therefore, in order to avoid alienating the masses, Hindu or Muslim, it is seen as being appropriate to bypass existing church structures. Seekers and converts are discipled in their own cultural milieu and not labelled as Chris-tian, simply being called followers of Christ. Fellowship and instructional needs are met through itinerant evangelists and teachers. In due season, as more response occurs in the vil-e or sub-caste or extended family, a small house church rges. Non-believers then are allowed to stumble over t, not over non-essentials of the faith that have to do with cultural application and personal choice. Thus the argument goes.

Can The Church Be Supra-Cultural?

How basic is culture to our self-understanding? Why is it that the more we become globalised, the more we retain our tribalisation? How does the church relate to culture? While recognising that we are asking huge questions which cannot be adequately dealt with in this book, we will take a stab at offering brief answers – if only to stimulate further reflection and debate. This is an extremely important theological issue, whether one is dealing with foreign missions or relating the church to the world in one's own culture.

The stubborn tenacity of culture is seen in the story of Lee Lai-Shan, who won an Olympic gold medal in windsurfing at the Atlanta games. She was the first athlete from Hong Kong ever to win an Olympic gold medal. Asked about whether there was any special significance in her being the first gold medallist and last for Hong Kong under British rule, she had a curious answer. Lee Lai-Shan blurted out: 'All I was thinking was how hard I'd trained the past several years. [Next time] I will still represent Hong Kong. Whether it is Britain or China is just [a] historical issue. I will still be a Hong Kong athlete.'[1] At the core, she retained 'tribal' loyalties. Identity at root was locally-derived.

Without getting into a lengthy consideration of how Gospel and culture relate, it is assumed here that the church is to be rooted in culture and to rise above culture. The Gospel came to earth via the Jewish culture, but as Peter's vision revealed, its expression was not to be understood as exclusively Jewish (Acts 10). Similarly, Christ the Word became flesh (was culturally-rooted in his humanity) and yet remained the eternal Word (remained above culture in his divinity) and so informs our understanding of how Gospel and culture relate. Lesslie Newbigin captures this need for balance in understanding w

---

[1] 'Smooth Sail Into History,' *Newsweek*. Dec. 30, 1996, p. 33.

when he says: 'There can never be a culture-free gospel. Yet the gospel, which is from the beginning to the end embodied in culturally conditioned forms, calls into question all cultures, including the one in which it was originally embodied.'[2] The church, then, by this interpretation of the relevant Scriptural data, is both supra-cultural and culturally-bound.

Critical Contextualisation

Missiologist Paul Hiebert makes an important contribution to the contextualisation debate in calling for missionaries to engage in 'critical contextualisation'.[3] Scripture is to be accepted as the final authority for truth but the local church is allowed to function as a 'hermeneutical community'. Local churches and the missionary gather and analyse all beliefs and customs, first in terms of their meaning within their own cultural setting, and then in terms of biblical norms. It is deemed important for the local church to make the final decision as to whether the custom under scrutiny is to be retained or rejected.[4] Indigenous theologies may address issues that Western minds have bypassed because of their own cultural presuppositions. These fit into what Hiebert calls the 'excluded middle'. Examples of this excluded middle include spirit world forces which may be phenomenologically observed but which don't fit the standard 'scientific' criteria for inclusion in worldviews as understood by Westerners. If Hiebert's paradigm for doing mission is correct, then it would seem that globalisation forces can be an impediment to, or at least must take a back seat to, contextualisation, for they will prevent nationals in leadership of the emerging church from applying Scripture in their own way to their own culture. Theologising, then, must cut two ways. It must not only have one foot in the biblical revelation

Lesslie Newbigin, *Foolishness To the Greeks: The Gospel and Western Culture* (Grand Rapids, MI: William B. Eerdmans Publishing Co., 1989), p. 4.

Paul Hiebert, *Anthropological Reflections on Theological Issues* (Grand Rapids, Baker Book House, 1994).

Paul Hiebert, *Anthropological Insights for Missionaries* (Grand Rapids, MI: Baker Book House, 1994), p. 187.

and the other foot in the historico-cultural context of the missionary, but it must also must return to the biblical revelation and work back to the historical and cultural context of the people being reached with the Gospel.

At the same time, it must be noted that Hiebert's stress on the hermeneutical community as interpreter of Truth leaves unresolved the question of where universals intersect cultural variables, the former leading to formal correspondence in the global church and the latter leading to dynamic equivalence locally. It is fine, the argument can be made, to have a high view of culture, but is God hostage to culture in mediating eternal truth or does he use it uniquely as a vehicle in communicating his intended revelation? Does not the grammatico-historical method make possible in most cases the correct understanding of the text, or is the missionary so influenced by his or her own culture (as Kraft would have it) that he or she is unable to objectively interpret Truth to the receptor culture? These are not new questions and the purpose of this chapter is as much to acknowledge the questions as it is to suggest a resolution to age-old problems.[5] Humility is the order of the day because missionaries have been baffled by this missiological challenge since the Jerusalem church had to rule on Jewish to Gentile implanting of the Gospel in Acts 15!

As we seek clarification of how Gospel and culture intersect let us turn to Newbigin's profound statement:

> The Bible is not a collection of documents recently dug up in the sands of Egypt. It is quite 'unscientific' to treat it as if it were. The Bible comes into our hands as the book of a community, and neither the book nor the community are properly understood except in their reciprocal relationship with each other. Quite clearly, the community as it now exists is being continuously shaped by the attention it gives to the Bible. Equally clearly, the community's reading of the Bible is shaped by a tradition that has been developed through the experience of previous genera-tions of believers in seeking to understand and put in

[5] For a good summary of the contextualisation debate, see David J. Hessel and Edward Rommen, *Contextualisation: Meanings, Methods, and Models* (Rapids, MI: Baker Book House, 1992).

practice the meaning of the book. The 'pre-understanding' with which the contemporary community comes to its reading of the Bible is shaped by the ways in which previous generations of Christians have come to understand it in the course of their discipleship. Every Christian reader comes to the Bible with the spectacles provided by the tradition that is alive in the community to which he or she belongs, and that tradition is being constantly modified as each new generation of believers endeavours to be faithful in understanding and living out Scripture. This is the hermeneutical circle operating within the believing community.[6]

To revisit the example with which we started this discussion, proponents of a more contextualised approach to church planting among Hindus and Muslims in India decry any effort to encourage converts to leave their communal setting, hence the concept of churchless Christianity referred to above. 'Extraction evangelism' would require converts to relate to an existing church. This strategy is accused of being the cause of a lack of breakthrough in India's close-knit communities.[7]

But from my conversation with such converts, I realise it is not easy to come to the conclusion that most of them have left home due to the misplaced strategy of the missionary or national Christian who may have been instrumental in their conversion. Rather, many of them have found that they have been unable to practise their faith with integrity, being true to their own understanding of Scripture, while remaining a functioning part of their caste or extended family structure. They have seen no or little difference between many forms and their functions.[8] An example of a failure to distinguish between form

---

[6] Newbigin, *Foolishness*, pp. 55–56.
[7] H. L. Richard, 'Is Extraction Evangelism Still the Way To Go?' *Mission Frontiers Bulletin* (September-October, 1996): 14–16.
Anthropologists rightly distinguish between *forms* and their meanings in analysing a society. Christians do the same sort of thing in distinguishing biblical principles from cultural applications of those principles (e.g., as in the wearing of head coverings by women in the church at Corinth versus the principle of doing things decently and in order in the context of corporate worship). Charles may say that 'Christianness lies primarily in the functions served and the meanings conveyed by the cultural forms employed, rather than in the forms themselves . . . God seeks to use and to cooperate with human beings in the

and function that can only cause unnecessary alienation is the refusing of Indian Christians to allow their brides to wear red – the Hindu custom, symbolising fertility; instead insisting on white, representing purity, but standing for infertility and death within Hinduism. These converts say that to remain in their native community without breaking caste is difficult in that it will no doubt involve too much compromise. It is the position taken here that this puzzlement remains unresolved in the evangelical community and needs further study and prayer. The issues are being raised without being answered in this chapter. Hopefully through raising them we can begin to search for answers.

Does Globalisation Equal Westernisation?

Perhaps the most serious indictment against globalisation in relation to planting the church cross-culturally is the charge that it is really purveying Western culture and not just facilitating the proclamation of the Gospel. For instance, K. C. Abraham argues cogently that globalisation is a process whereby the economies of different countries are aligned to the needs of several hundred multinational corporations and financial institutions like the World Bank and the International Monetary Fund.[9] Speaking disparagingly of this development, he says, '[Globalisation] is rooted in the culture of capitalism, whose predominant logic of development is profit-making ... [and is] the vehicle for cultural invasion [in which] the idea of progress is decisively shaped by Western lifestyle and its structures.'[10] Similarly, Peter Berger contends that globalisation is essentially the spread of certain vital economic, political, cultural, or

---

[8] *(continued)* continued use of relative cultural forms to express absolute supracultural meaning.' Quoted in Edward Rommen and Gary Corwin, eds *Missiology and the Social Sciences: Contributions Cautions, and Conclusion* (Pasadena, CA: William Carey Library, 1996), p. 38.
[9] K. C. Abraham, 'Globalization: A Gospel and Culture Perspective,' *Internati⟨* *Review of Mission* 85(336) (January, 1996): 87.
[10] *Ibid.*, pp. 87–88.

technological institutions of Western modernisation to the rest of the world.[11]

In a withering attack on globalisation in relation to the need for contextualisation in mission, a Caucasian ex-patriate in India who shall be left unnamed to protect his ministry among high caste Hindus, made these comments:

> [This organisation] by its very nature is a mighty force for building up the new international urbanised neo-western culture. Our globalisation will inevitably move in this direction . . . To counter this, which has a massive weight of historical and economic momentum, might be an impossible task . . . The rise of this new international culture is presented as a *help* toward internationalising, with no recognition of the serious problems involved. . . . What we need is a mighty thrust in the direction of *particular cultures.* . . . It seems to me that this whole issue of globalisation has only been seriously considered from an administrative point of view which must be considered an error of such great magnitude that it skews the entire process. A few of us have tried to raise the issue of ramifications or lack thereof on field ministries, but these issues seem to have been ignored.[12]

It is not just theologians and missiologists who decry the Westernisation that globalisation engenders. So do secular observers of cultural trends. M. P. Shamala is typical of Two-Thirds World journalists in lamenting the pervasiveness of Western influences in globalisation. He argues that new technologies of communication are multiplying the dangers of cultural domination by the technologically rich countries, which happen to be Western.[13] While the profit motive of multinational corporations may transcend national interests, the language and culture of these globalised companies is still largely American.

ter Berger, *Religion and Globalization* (London: Sage Publications, 1994), -9.

en from a letter to the author of July 11, 1994.

. Shamala, 'Globalisation and the Media,' *The Hindu Magazine*, Sunday, 8, 1995.

In pondering the impact of globalisation on missions, it can be argued that national leaders of emerging churches in the Two-Thirds World are thoroughly Westernised and form a worldwide subculture that causes them to be somewhat alienated from their own people. Often educated abroad, used to high living (by local standards), and more comfortable in English than their mother tongue, these Two-Thirds World Christian leaders often have trouble relating the Gospel to their neighbours, let alone the local Christian community. Such is the criticism levelled against some of the leaders of the church in India.

But critics of the church in India further maintain that the church's relative inability to make a substantial impact on society has a lot to do with its 'foreignness'. Christians there may be more familiar with the American evangelical financial consultant Larry Burkett than they are with the Indian self-help guru Deepak Chopra. Indian pastors mimic British expositional preachers rather than learning to weave the narrative and parabolic style of the Bible into their sermons, which would suit their own culture so well. Maranatha Praise tapes are best-sellers while native-style tapes featuring tabla and sitar wither on the vine. And so the Indian church is perceived as being neither Indian nor foreign. It is viewed as being yet another caste. All globalisation seems to have done is isolate Indian Christians from the millions of caste Hindus who form a monolithic bloc of humanity sealed off from meaningful contact with Christians who fit into their context.

But then again, is not the acknowledgement of the existence of a neo-Western subculture important in our understanding of today's complex world? After all does caste Hinduism really represent a monolithic religio-cultural reality? We have already referred to the Westernising influences of globalisation on India in entertainment, communications, and management styles. Caste Hindus are the ones leading the way in computer software development, for example. They are not donning the saffron robes of the sannyasi (who renounce the world and on a spiritual pilgrimage in large numbers in defiance of consumerism and individualism of the globalised world). might in fact question whether the tight-knit communal s of caste Hinduism survives intact anywhere except in Indian village life. Urbanisation has also had a leavening affect on this traditional Indian society. There's always a danger of taking our understanding of world religions from classical textbook descriptions of them rather than through observing their popular practice. Hence, we find that Bhakti Hinduism is more of a driving force among the masses than Advaita Hinduism. Superstition and Sufism play a more powerful role in Islam than orthodox expressions. Besides, to refocus on Indian Christians, what's wrong with them possessing their own distinctive culture, which is neither fully Indian nor fully foreign? That's the way the church has evolved, for better or for worse, so let Indian evangelicals accept themselves and feel comfortable with who they are. When it comes to interacting critically with the larger culture, though, like churches in all societies, they will have to 'learn a new language' and make some costly and painful adjustments.

This complexity of modern society has been well described by Jonathan Ingleby in a missiological article questioning the neutrality of 'contextualisation'.[14] When we take the Gospel across cultures, he asks, do we not oversimplify the receptor culture, when in fact we are confronted with a variety of cultures? Missionaries then must make a choice about which culture(s) to recognise, which to focus on, and how to go about their work. Ingleby further goes on to say that it is the dominant culture and not the marginalised culture which usually gets the quality attention. It might be conjectured that globalised mission forces will tend to be well-financed and affluent (in comparison with those being reached) and thus, perhaps unconsciously, find it easier to select the aspect of the local culture that they understand best or have the most affinity with, and ascribe to the whole what is really true only in the part, hence skewing any effective contextualisation.

All this goes to show that there is little that is black-and-white in contextualisation matters. It behoves both

---

Jonathan Ingleby, 'Trickling Down or Shaking the Foundations: Is Contextualization Neutral?' *Missiology: An International Review* 25(2)) (April, 183–187.

globalisation proponents and contextualisation proponents to refrain from being dogmatic about their positions while at the same time continuing to take the Gospel to unreached peoples in a spirit of learning and flexibility about how these two vital aspects of missions are to coexist. Advocates of globalisation must defend themselves against the charge that they are too fascinated with the quantitative side of missions: How many missionaries can we get into the people group or country? What resources will it take to reach the goal we have set for ourselves to plant so many churches by a certain date? Aren't most problems reducible to managing or marketing issues? Advocates of contextualisation must answer the charge that they are too qualitative-oriented in doing mission: What accommodation can be made to the culture instead of seeing the transforming nature of Gospel and its proclamation? Isn't discipling more important than the number of converts? Isn't the social dimension of mission as important as the spiritual? We need to learn from each other in areas where the Bible, and our application of its message, is unclear. Reconciling globalisation and contextualisation is one such example.

ELEVEN

The Future of Globalisation in Missions

The provocative title of the *Newsweek* magazine article, *'What Color Is Black?'* did not disappoint.[1] It delivered a stimulating, albeit unsettling, message. Basically, the thesis of the article was that there has been so much intermarrying racially over the years and so much immigration in the last three decades in America, that the old racially drawn lines were no longer so easy to establish. The same argument could hold true for any number of Western World countries. For example, in 1992, Great Britain had about six hundred thousand South Asians.[2] Canada had five hundred thousand South Asians.[3] Some intermarriage is occurring between South Asians and the mainstream population in both countries. Certainly, caste-based marriages are no longer a foregone conclusion as they would be back in South Asia. Both these factors are typical of the ones complicating the issue of race and skin pigmentation of offspring in today's modern cities the world over.

If race is determined by skin pigmentation, the argument goes, the two-way definition of what race is (e.g., black versus white) no longer has merit. What colour is black, for instance? If you look at a cross-section of Britons or Americans today it is

Tom Morganthau, 'What Color Is Black?', *Newsweek*. February 15, 1995, 47–49.

ted in Margaret Wardell and Ram Gidoomal, *Chapatis For Tea* (Guilford, y: Highland Books, 1994), p. 2.

h Asians are people living in or coming from India, Pakistan, Bangla- ri Lanka, and Nepal.

every shade and hue from tan to ebony you will see and before you know it the politics of pigmentation are up for grabs decades after the Montgomery bus boycott or the Gandhian South African protest.

Then when you consider the current scientific findings on biological variations within the human species, you discover that there isn't any significant set of differences which distinguishes one colour of people from another.[4] Physiological features that exist as a result of inter-marriage: thin lips, brown eyes, big ears, hooked noses are continuing to blur as the world urbanises and globalises. This is an over-simplification of the debate among biologists, anthropologists, and sociologists about ethnicity and race, but the fact remains that the way we see the world and each other is being profoundly altered by the reality of globalisation.

The 'sameness' of life around the world, especially in pop culture, is astounding. *Newsweek*, in its end of the year issue for 1996, called it the 'colonisation of the planet' by American culture, particularly by Hollywood. Not surprisingly, then, 80 per cent of viewers tune in to the *X-Files* in English, in Hong Kong on Tuesday evenings. In China, you can buy Chicago Bulls' shirts in the bazaar. One in ten British watch TV's dysfunctional American family, *The Simpsons*. Russians watch *Sesame Street* with regularity. Egyptians sport Oakland Raiders' football jerseys. Iranians risk life and limb selling forbidden Hollywood videos in suitcases door-to-door. In some respects, culture wars, in which individual ethnic groups are seeking to preserve their ways of life and distinctives vis-à-vis globalisation trends, are a lost cause.

Sophisticated tastes emerging in the Two-Thirds World only exacerbate the globalisation trend. Young women of South-East Asia are brand conscious. These brand names are not local ones either. Chanel handbags or Disney kids' outfits reveal that the appetite is there to experience the lifestyles of the rich and famous.[5] 'If you take a typical Indian teenager in Bombay, Delh or Calcutta, you would find that tangibly he has moved towa

---

[4] Sharon Begley, 'There Is Not Enough', *Newsweek*, February 15, 199⁵ 50–52.
[5] Naisbitt, *Megatrends*, p. 93.

the West,' maintains the director of Parle Agro, a Bombay seller of a boxed fruit drink called Frooty. 'He'd be wearing a Lacoste shirt, Wrangler jeans, Nike shoes, and maybe a pair of Ray-Ban glasses,' says Jagdeep Kapoor.[6]

Asian Driven

Could John Naisbitt be correct when he claims in *Megatrends Asia* that what is happening in Asia today is the most important development in the world? He predicts that global companies must have at least a third of their business in Asia to remain dominant in their fields.[7] His compilations show him that if the Asian middle class continues its 6 to 10 per cent annual expansion rate of the nineties, the Asian middle class, not including Japan, could number between eight hundred million and one billion by 2010. This will result in an astonishing $8 trillion to $10 trillion in spending money, which would be roughly the equivalent of 50 per cent more than today's US economy.[8] We would be putting our heads in the sand if we were to think that the economic Asian Flu will indefinitely postpone the ascendancy of Asian economies.

Naisbitt is not the only one trumpeting the potential of Asia. When Rupert Murdoch, owner of one of the world's vastest communications' networks, purchased *Star TV*, he extended his tentacles into Asia, enabling his empire to gird all continents except Africa. With the purchase of *Star* in 1993, he instantly had an audience of forty-five million viewers in thirteen million homes across Asia. His acquisition was not an accident, for his theory is that for the foreseeable future the world economy is likely to boom only in Asia.[9]

The greatest remaining bloc of unreached peoples in the world is in Asia too. Two of the largest missionary-sending countries are in Asia: Korea and India. China has the second most evangelicals of any one nation in the world, at least fifty

---

[6] *Ibid.*, p.112.
[7] *Ibid.*, p.18.
[8] *Ibid.*, p.89.
[9] William Shawcross, *Murdoch* (New York: Simon & Shuster, 1994), p. 8.

million strong. The potential of that one national church for world evangelisation (and its own evangelisation) is unlimited should China politically liberalise in the same way as it has been doing economically. Yes, we can expect a paradigm shift. Europe and North America will not be the centre of Christianity nor of missions. The privilege of that position will shift to Asia, closely followed by Latin America and Africa.

Feeling At Home Anywhere

The story has been told of how the Tuareg Muslim tribesmen of North Africa have in recent years delayed their annual camel caravan across the Sahara in order to watch an episode of *Dallas*.[10] As we saw in our chapter on contextualisation, the homogenisation that comes with globalisation can be both a strength and weakness, having synergistic impact and yet being an Achilles heel too. The world's post-nationalism, the levelling of hierarchies through networking, and the standardisation of certain aspects of culture, have resulted in a reinforcing of globalisation tendencies. Thus we find intercultural management specialists like Ohmae insisting that 'in order to establish a truly global business, companies must view the world from a global perspective [with] people, systems, and organizational structures . . . reflect[ing] this perspective.'[11] OM and missions analogous to it must heed this global reality as they reflect on the power of their structures and values in creating a common organisational culture and vision.

Yet we have also been learning that in spite of this impetus toward globalisation, cultural identity and integrity can be preserved. That is to say, simultaneously, and paradoxically, this growing awareness of the profound interconnectedness of human life has also brought heightened sensitivity and attachment to the diversity of it. Theologian Max Stackhouse puts it this way: 'Certainly the processes of globalization disrupt fragile societies and disrupt traditional identities. But globalization

---

[10] *Ibid.*, p. 426.
[11] Ohmae, *Triad Power*, 1985, p. 209.

need not necessarily mean homogeneity. Indeed, in some respects, globalization fosters and allows for differences.'[12] He then offers two examples of what he means. One is that you can find ethnic foods in almost any town anywhere in the world. Indian mango pickle, for instance, finds shelf space in most British super markets. Another example is that tribal peoples are increasingly networking globally by fax and e-mail.

At the same time, we need to remember the point made earlier in the book that not only does globalisation not always hinder diversity but it does not destroy the virility of local culture (what Naisbitt calls tribalisation). To test the validity of this statement one only has to consider the difficulty multinational corporations face when choosing names for their transnational products. Some of the struggles in having internationally successful names are amusing. Take the Ford Pinto. In Brazil, *pinto* is a slang term meaning 'under-endowed male'. In Latin, *nova* means 'new star' (used for the Chevrolet Nova car) but when spoken aloud in Spanish, it sounds like *no va* – 'it doesn't go'. In Germany Puffs Tissues won't sell well with that name because it is a slang term for a brothel![13]

It is also a bit of a misnomer to insist that there are only a few multinational companies in the world which are controlling the vast majority of the world's Gross National Product and that they are largely American-based, so as to homogenise the world's culture, etc. In 1970, according to the UN Center on Transnationals, there were seven thousand multinational companies across the globe with more than half of them head-quartered either in Great Britain or the United States. But by the 1990s there were thirty-five thousand multinationals, with less than half of them being based in the United States, Japan, Germany, and Switzerland combined.[14]

Yet another aspect of the changing face of the global church and world missions, which will be beautiful to behold, is the networking of Two-Thirds Worlders with Two-Thirds

---

[12] Max Stackhouse, 'The Global Future and the Future of Globalization,' *Christian Century* 114(1) (Feb. 2–9, 1994): 109.
[13] Vince Beiser, 'The Corporate Name Game,' *Macleans*. (Jan. 12, 1998), pp. 28–30.
[14] Barnet and Cavanagh, *Dreams*, p. 423.

Worlders. Two-Thirds Worlders will not only feel increasingly at home with Westerners as equal partners; power will not only be diffused more within global entities; Two-Thirds Worlders will hunger for more models of leadership, of success in church planting among resistant peoples, of how to do mission from their own kind of people.

This bonding between South and South is powerfully illustrated in a story told by Chuck Bennett, president of Partners International. On his first trip to Africa, he had the opportunity to speak at a retreat for Christian leaders in Zimbabwe, back in the days when it was called Rhodesia and was beset by racial tensions. Immediately after his arrival he was asked quite unexpectedly to address the subject of church growth. Caught by surprise, he reverted to speaking about the strength of the fast-growing Christian movement in Mexico being in its lay volunteers and how God had overruled the many mistakes of the foreign missionaries. When he finished talking to his rapt audience of mostly Africans, the Africans began to ask questions. It suddenly occurred to him, as he answered the third question, that these black Africans, after hearing that Mexicans were not white, were going to apply everything he told them about their Mexican brethren, to their own churches. Bennett then observes: 'I concluded that this was the first time these African leaders had heard about churches they could relate to emotionally. Until then they had only heard idealized stories from white missionaries about churches in America and Great Britain.'[15] The perception is changing to that of seeing that 'all have bread to give and to receive.'[16]

Perhaps the paradigm shift is more that we no longer perceive the whole in terms of one of its parts. The parts are still very much in evidence. But the worldview has been radically resculptured to encompass the whole. In the words of Stanley Grenz, we are arriving at a 'global consciousness', which is

---

[15] The story is told in Chuck Bennett, *God in the Corners* (San Jose, CA: Partners International, 1997), pp. 64–66.
[16] James Chukwuma Okoye, ' "Mutual Exchange of Energies" Mission in Cross-Cultural Perspective: An African Point of View,' *Missiology: An International Review* 25(4) (Oct., 1997): 467.

irreversible.[17] On the practical level for mission agencies like OM this will mean holding in creative tension the pluralism and universalisation of this new reality. Asian theologians and mission leaders who think primarily in the thought processes and languages of the Western World must consciously distinguish between the two and ensure that methodologies and theologies are translated into the vernacular.[18] The local church will have to be esteemed alongside the universal church, the local culture alongside the global culture, contextualisation alongside globalisation.

So What Is a Globalised Mission Agency?

Just what shape should we expect an international mission agency to take, in which diversity and unity are exhibited so as to reflect the true parameters of globalisation? It may have been surmised by this juncture that there are a variety of possibilities. The most frequent model used has been OM. But there are other possible versions whereby global partnerships in missions can swing into action. Ones that come to mind are as follows:

1. *Joint venture between semi-independent partners*

OM would be an example of this type of partnership. Whether for legal or philosophical reasons, each national wing (field) of OM is semi-autonomous. OM-Canada is registered in Canada with the federal government as an independent, registered charity with its own board of directors. If OM-Canada perceives itself as part of a worldwide family or organisation, that is incidental as far as the government is concerned. As far as the Canadian government is concerned, the only way OM-Canada can be connected with OM internationally is if it enters into a joint venture or ministry agreement with her as a collection of

---

[17] Stanley Grenz, 'Community as a Theological Motif for the Western Church in an Era of Globalization,' *Crux* 28(3) (Sept., 1992): 10.
[18] Kosuke Koyama, 'Theological Education: Its Unities and Diversities,' *Theological Education* 30(1) (Autumn, 1993): 104.

autonomous, duly recognised charities, while allowing OM-Canada to retain its independence. Nevertheless, OM internationally works around these complexities so as to maintain a genuine form of worldwide organisational integrity. Funds are commingled, common principles and practices are observed, consensus on mission and vision statements is achieved, and deployment of human resources in a coherent and co-ordinated fashion is made possible. Yet simultaneously, a fair degree of local autonomy is realised. Indigenisation exists at the national level in many locations.[19]

2. Joint venture between fully independent partners

Often this type of arrangement will take the form of one organisation providing funds for another mission in the country in which a mutually desirable ministry is sought. Examples of this sort of arrangement are: Tear Fund, Partners International, and Gospel For Asia.[20]

3. Vertically integrated networking of independent partners

Phill Butler, of Interdev, an agency serving as a catalyst in forging mission partnerships on the international level, has articulated the concept of a partnership which he calls 'vertically integrated'.[21] This occurs when a combination of organisations co-operate in a one-time or an ongoing project which targets an unreached people, so that previous difficulties are surmounted through the pooling of individual strengths in such areas as prayer, financing, strategising, providing of skilled workers, and training. An example of this sort of partnership would be the United Mission To Nepal.[22]

---

[19] For further discussion of this sort of global mission organisation see Hicks, pp. 15, 22 on OM, and Tebbe in Taylor, *Kingdom*, 1994, pp. 138–140 on InterServe.

[20] For further information on this sort of partnership see Bush and Lotz, *Partnering*, 1990, p. 6, Pate in Kraakevik and Welliver, *Partners* p. 172, Keyes and Pate, *Missiology*, 1994, pp. 13–15, Keyes and Pate, *Missiology*, p. 204.

[21] Phill Butler, 'Why Strategic Partnerships?: A Look At New Strategies For Evangelism,' in J. Kraakevik and D. Welliver, p. 169.

[22] For further discussion of this sort of partnership see Taylor, *Kingdom*, 1994, pp. 13–15, Keyes and Pate, *Missiology*, pp. 204–205.

Butler reports that over the last twelve years his agency has developed twenty-five strategic evangelism partnerships to penetrate unreached people groups, with another twenty-five partnerships in the works. These partnerships involve 225 mission agencies from more than thirty countries, with nearly 30 per cent of them being non-Western.[23]

4. *Informal association between independent agencies*

This kind of arrangement occurs especially in 'creative-access' countries where only a few missionaries, often in the form of tentmakers, are found. Because their ability to minister freely is seriously curtailed, there is often an unofficial networking of missionaries by virtue of necessity, regardless of organisational affiliation. An instance of this sort of co-operation would be the way Arab World Ministries, Frontiers, Gospel Missionary Union, and other groups link up in Morocco. When Two-Thirds World agencies enter this scenario, the globalisation of missions is all the more profound.

Come what may, the purest form of globalisation in missions happens when Western World and Two-Thirds World entities work together bilaterally, and in such a way that there is a sense of equal partnership, in decision making, planning, and sharing of core values, without one partner dominating the other. Where nationalities blend together in the same organisation, on the other hand, we can call the organisation globalised only when it is predisposed to shed its Western-dominated internal values, structures, and leadership. Otherwise it is simply an international organisation, without being globalised.

Grass Roots Missionaries

Sunny is an Indian evangelist with OM in India.[24] Sunny is a rare breed: a convert from Islam. He has a burden to reach his own people. Imagine his excitement then, when one day while

---

[23] Phill Butler, 'An Open Letter To North America's Mission Agency Leadership,' *Mission Frontiers Bulletin* Sept.-Oct., 1996: 26.
[24] This story is taken from *OM India News*, [summer 1996], p. 5.

cycling through a village, he saw a *maulana* (a Muslim religious leader), sitting cross-legged in a tea shop poring over a New Testament. Sunny dismounted, went into the tea shop and started a conversation.

'What are you reading?' he asked.

'I am reading a holy book, the New Testament. I bought it in a bookshop for three rupees', the man answered.

'Why are you reading this book?', countered Sunny.

The *maulana*, whose name was Ahmed, sat back in his chair, closed his eyes, and exclaimed, 'I don't want to be blind. When I read the Koran, I don't get any answers.' Astoundingly, he then turned to 2 Peter 3:18 and read, 'But grow in grace and in the knowledge of our Lord Jesus Christ.'

Sunny was then able to explain to Ahmed that he too had been brought up to be a religious instructor and had learned Arabic for that very reason. Sunny concluded by saying, 'I had the same questions you have, but now I have become a follower of Christ.' Ahmed's face lit up. He wanted to talk further. The two left the tea shop and sat under a nearby tree where they conversed for three more hours. Sunny now meets Ahmed regularly and they read the Bible together. Another *maulana* is also studying the New Testament.

There are over one hundred million Muslims in India, more than in any other single country except Indonesia. Who will reach them? I suspect, if the track record of the modern missionary movement is any indication, that it will not be primarily Western missionaries. Instead, it may very well be grass roots nationals like Sunny. They may turn the tide in the unreached world of over one billion Muslims. For one thing, there are still simply too many unreached people to leave the task of evangelisation solely to missionaries from the West. According to David Barrett's 1997 'Annual Statistical Table on Global Mission', in mid-1997 there were 3,897 million non-Christians, a group that is growing by 47 million per year, or, at an increase of 129,000 per day.[25]

---

[25] Published in the *International Bulletin of Missionary Research* each year, this number cited in January, 1997 edition, pp. 24–25.

If trends reported on recently by Robert Coote are indicative of the future, there will be a marked decline in the contribution of missionaries to 'the Cause' from the Western World in the first decade of the twenty-first century, at least if measured in terms of career missionaries.[26] Impressions of rapid growth of North American missionaries have been fuelled, as it turns out, by including the number of short-term missionaries in totals which until the last two decades were mainly the privy of career missionaries. Another observation Coote makes is that the growth in numbers of North American missionaries has not kept pace in the last twenty-five years with the rate of population increase either in North America or of the least reached regions of the world. All the more reason, then, why a clarion call should go to the Two-Thirds World churches to join the battle.

Globalisation of missions may enable the worldwide church to bring closure to the fulfilment of the Great Commission in this generation. That is the thrust of the first chapter, where different mission eras are described, with it being the conjecture made there that the rise of the Two-Thirds World missionary force could very well be the final of four great eras in modern missionary history. In this vein, Luis Bush, as spokesperson for GCOWE '95, a planet-wide gathering of mission and church leaders in Korea, organised to strategise and pray over the goal of seeing a church established for every people and the Gospel available for every person by AD 2000, made these assumptions:

> The realization [is] that when the whole church is mobilized, there is much greater probability that the whole world will be reached. . . . Because of the explosive growth of the Two-Thirds World church in this century, the global church is positioned for a major evangelistic thrust in the nineties. . . . Many church and mission leaders now believe that genuine partnerships is [sic.] the only way to

[26] Robert Coote, 'Good News, Bad News: North American Protestant Overseas Personnel Statistics in Twenty-Five Year Perspective,' *International Bulletin of Missionary Research* January, 1995: 6–12.

take advantage of the opportunities presented by this last decade of the century.[27]

If one can put a thousand to flight and two put ten thousand to flight (Deut. 32:30), the new synergy in missions created by globalisation may surely usher in missions' final era. At what point Matthew 24:14 will be fulfilled in terms of world evangelisation, we don't know, but the nascent era of national missionaries may be the final piece of the puzzle put in place to pave the way for Christ's return (cf. 2 Pet. 3:12).

Limits of Change

It is important to be realistic about the speed with which organisational change can occur to adjust to the reality of globalisation. Missions trying to reconfigure to take into account the fact of globalisation – beware! Students of organisational change uniformly caution against expecting that needed change to happen quickly, without wholesale upheaval and negative ramifications.[28] One of the reasons for the slow rate of organisational change is the same reason why some people avoid counselling: they are afraid of the insights that counselling usually brings, insights which might force them to effect radical and often painful behavioural change. As Western missionaries and churches adjust values, customs, and mindsets to accommodate Two-Thirds World brothers and sisters as equal partners in the cause of world evangelisation, we must resist any tendency to settle for snail-paced change, even if at the same time we want to avoid change that is too rapid; change must not be perceived as loss. The realisation must dawn that true partnership does not diminish value, but adds it. Pickard speaks of this synergy when he says, 'True partnerships . . . do not take away; they add to and strengthen the hands of member partners.'[29]

---

[27] Bush, *Funding*, 1993, pp. 2–3.
[28] Deal and Kennedy, *Corporate Cultures*, 1982, pp. 161–162; Schein, *Organizational Culture*, pp. 305–312; Senge, *The Fifth Discipline*.
[29] David Pickard, 'Partnership in Mission: OMF in a Unique China Partnership.' in Taylor, p. 192.

While an effort has been attempted herein to make the pathway clearer for those involved in the task of world evangelisation, it is difficult to know where exactly the path will lead. So much happens in the overall environment over which mission strategists have no control: War, Demographic patterns, Disease, Political Upheaval – to name a few factors which will most obviously impinge on globalisation efforts. Nationalism, economics, and pluralism will also continue to make the pathway of globalisation in missions unpredictable.

A Foretaste of Heaven

The most exhilarating spiritual experience I have had has occurred several times when I have been present at a massive gathering of OM workers from many parts of the world, as we were caught up in corporate worship. This experience seemed to me to be a foretaste of heaven where 'a great multitude that no one can count, from every nation, tribe, people and language' (Rev. 7:9–10) will be collected before the throne of God. Down on planet earth, this sort of happening is made possible by the globalisation of mission – not just in terms of the end result of a church for every people, but as missionaries work side by side from a wide variety of nations.

Globalisation of missions enables the missionary movement to demonstrate to the world the catholicity and the unity of the Body of Christ. It enables the church to model impartiality and partnership. It releases servanthood and stewardship for the sake of the spread of the Gospel. It unleashes Kingdom ministry at its best. Samuel Escobar eloquently captures this vision in the following observation:

> The world to come at the end of history will be a world without the national barriers that divide people today, a glorious and rich mosaic of peoples, languages, and cultures around the Lamb of God. Missionary internationalization is a clear step in that direction.[30]

---

[30] Escobar, Speech, 1991.

As globalisation of missions emerges, we see a maturation in relationships occurring that is at the heart of Kingdom-forged relationships. The Body of Christ is not to function as a collection of individuals, but as a unit characterised by interdependence. While national churches and missionary movements must assert their own independence and indigeneity, they must not lose sight of the fact that they have received a blessing in order to be a blessing to others. To be a blessing to the larger world at some point in time will require them to make the transition from independence to interdependence. Synergetic partnerships within the global Body of Christ will be necessary to further 'the Cause'. Years ago, E. Stanley Jones understood this maturation cycle when he remarked, 'Suppose all nations get their freedom, will that be the end? No, for that would bring us only to the second stage of human development – the stage of interdependence. The stage of interdependence is the stage of maturity for nations as well as individuals'.[31] The blossoming of this interdependence can only glorify God at the same time as it hastens the completion of the task of world evangelisation. Lesslie Newbigin put it this way: 'The movement of missionaries [should be] multidirectional, all churches both sending and receiving. The Word of God is to be spoken in every tongue, but it can never be domesticated in any.'[32] We need each other in order to comprehend Christ in all his greatness (Eph. 3:14ff.) and to complete world evangelisation.

Conclusion

If we can conceptualise the process of grappling with globalisation organisationally, like looking at a photograph, perhaps we will have insight into what this book has been all about. When one cuts up a photograph, each part reveals only a section of the whole picture. Likewise, when one generalises about globalisation by considering only one or two of its aspects, one is like the person taking only a portion of a photograph and thinking he or she is seeing the whole picture. We have sought to

---

[31] E. Stanley Jones, *Christian Maturity* (Nashville, Abingdon, 1980), p. 215.

[32] Newbigin, *Foolishness*, p. 147.

look at globalisation holistically. After all, it is something of a construct, with many different ways of considering it and many different factors to keep in mind when seeking to understand it.

Where true globalisation has taken place, each part of the organisation or ministry is distinctive and yet clearly imaging the whole. When the parts are woven together, they don't change the nature of the photograph as a whole. But they do make it come more alive. Such is the synergy fashioned by true global partnerships. This synergy is what Covey has in mind in his statement that 'sameness is not oneness; uniformity is not unity. Unity, or oneness, is complementariness, not sameness. Sameness is uncreative . . . and boring. The essence of synergy is to value the differences.'[33]

Peter Maiden, OM's Associate International Director, shall have the last word. In a personal letter to me of November 15, 1994, he philosophised wistfully about a new day in OM saying:

> When I speak of globalising the organisation [OM], I look forward to the day when Indians, Latins, Africans, etc. can feel as comfortable and at home in our Area and International gatherings as Westerners do. I also look forward to the day when our meetings are conducted in a way which enables people from non-Western cultures to play a full part in our discussions. I recognise the danger of creating in OM a neo-Western culture and we want to avoid that at all cost.

May we keep in step with the Spirit as he does a new thing in seeking to win a people for himself from all over the world through globalisation of missions. May the modern missionary movement (now encompassing the whole church in the whole world) be like the Great Banyan Tree preserved in the Botanical Gardens in Calcutta. Two hundred years ago, somewhere in the middle of a massive tree measuring 1251 feet in circumference, the central trunk began. Now it no longer really supports the sprawling growth of this tent-like phenomenon, having been hollowed out by fungus damage years ago. Underneath

---

[33] Covey, *7 Habits*, p. 274.

the banyan tree, shade and protection from the elements are found so that life can go on. Such, we trust, will be the legacy of the globalisation of missions, the enriching and perpetuating of God's purposes for this planet.

Selected Bibliography

Adler, Nancy J. *International Dimensions of Organizational Behaviour*. Boston: PWS-Kent, 1991.

Allen, Roland. *Missionary Methods: St. Paul's or Ours?* London: World Dominion Press, 1930.

Azariah, V. S. *Christian Giving*. New York: Associated Press, 1955.

Barnet, Richard J., and Cavanagh, John. *Global Dreams: Imperial Corporations and the New World Order*. New York, NY: Simon & Schuster, 1994.

Berger, Peter. *Religion and Globalization*. London: Sage Publications, 1994.

Beyerhaus, Peter. 'The Three-Selves Formula – Is It Built On Biblical Foundations?' *International Review of Missions* 10 (1964):393–407.

Bonk, Jon. 'Globalization and Mission Education.' *Theological Education* 30(1) (Autumn 1993): 75.

Bonk, Jon, *Missions and Money*. Maryknoll, NY: Orbis Books, 1990.

Bosch, David. *Transforming Mission*: Paradigm Shifts in Theology of Mission Maryknoll, NY: Orbis Books, 1996.

Buhlmann, Walter. *The Coming of the Third Church*. Maryknoll, NY: Orbis Books, 1977.

Bush, Luis. *Funding Third World Missions*. Wheaton, IL: World Evangelical Fellowship Missions Committee, 1990.

Bush, Luis, and Lutz, Lorry. *Partnering in Ministry: The Direction of World Evangelism*. Downer's Grove, IL: Inter Varsity Press, 1990.

Cho, Y. J. and David H. Greenlee, 'Multinational Teams in Interantional Missions: A Reflection on American and Korean Cultural Values' (Unpublished paper by students at Trinity Evangelical Divinity School, 1990).

Conn, Harvey. 'The Money Barrier Between Sending and Receiving Churches.' *Evangelical Missions Quarterly* 14(4) (October 1978): 233, 235.

Coote, Robert. 'Good New, Bad News: North American Protestant Overseas Personnel Statistics in Twenty-Five Year Perspective.' *Internation Bulletin of Missionary Research* (January 1995): 6–12.

Deal, Terrance E. and Kennedy, Allan A. *Corporate Cultures: The Rites and Rituals of Corporate Life*. Reading, PA: Addison-Wesley, 1982.

Dodd, C. H. *Dynamics of Intercultural Communication*. Dubusque, IA: W. C. Brown, 1987.

Elmer, Duane. *Cross-Cultural Conflict: Building Relationships For Effective Ministry*. Downer's Grove, IL: InterVarsity Press, 1993.

Escobar, Samuel. 'The Internationalization of Missions and Leadership Style.' (speech to the 1991 EFMA Annual Convention).

Fernando, Ajith. ' "Rich" and "Poor" Nations and the Christian Enterprise: Some Personal Comments.' *Missiology: An International Review* 9(3) (July 1981): 287–298.

Fisher, Glen. *Mindsets*. Yarmouth, ME: Sage Publishing, 1988.

Fong, Bruce. 'Addressing the Issue of Racial Reconciliation According to the Principles of Eph. 2: 11–22.' *Journal of the Evangelical Theological Society* 38(4) (December 1995).

Frank, Sergei. 'Negotiating – An Underestimated Skill.' *Silver Kris* (December 1993): 34–38.

Glasser, Arthur; Hiebert, Paul; Wagner, Peter; and Winter, Ralph. *Crucial Dimensions of World Evangelization*. Pasadena, CA: William Carey Library, 1976.

Grenz, Stanley. 'Community as a Theological Motif for the Western Church in an Era of Globalization.' *Crux* 28(3) (September, 1992): 10.

Hall, E. T. *Beyond Culture*. Garden City, NY: Anchor, 1976.

Hall, E. T. *The Hidden Dimension*. Garden City, NY: Doubleday, 1966.

Hall, E. T. *The Silent Language*. Garden City, NY: Doubleday, 1959.

Hamm, P. 'Breaking the Power Habit: Imperative For Multinational Missions.' *Evangelical Missions Quarterly* 19(3): 180–189.

Harris, P. R. and Moran, R. T. *Managing Cultural Differences*. Houston: Gulf Publishing, 1987.

Hedlund, Roger. *Evangelisation and Church Growth: IssuesFrom the Asian Context*. Madras: McGavran Institute, 1992.

Hiebert, Paul. *Anthropological Reflections On Theological Issues*. Grand Rapids, MI: Baker Book House, 1994.

Hiebert, Paul. *Anthropological Insights For Missionaries*. Grand Rapids, MI: Baker Book House, 1994.

Hofstede, G. *Culture's Consequences: International Differences in Work-Related Values*. Beverley Hills, CA: Sage Publishers, 1984.

Ingleby, Jonathan. 'Trickling Down or Shaking the Foundations: Is Contextualization Neutral?' *Missiology: An International Review* 25(2) (April 1997): 183–187.

Johnstone, Patrick. *Operation World*. 5th ed. Grand Rapids, MI: Zondervan, 1993.

Keyes, Larry. *The Last Age of Missions*. Pasadena, CA: William Carey Library, 1983.

Keyes, Larry, and Pate, Larry. 'Two-Thirds World Missions: The Next 100 Years.' *Missiology: An International Review* 21(2): 187–206.

Koyama, Kosuke. 'Theological Education: Its Unities and Diversities.' *Theological Education* 30(1) (Autumn, 1993): 104.

Kraakevik, James H. and Welliver, Dotsey, eds. *Partners in the Gospel*. Wheaton, IL: The Billy Graham Center, 1991.

Kraft, Charles, and Wisley, T. N., eds. *Readings in Dynamic Indigenity*. Pasadena, CA: William Carey Library, 1979.

Kvin, P. 'The Magic of Multinational Management.' *Harvard Business Review* (November–December 1972).

Lingenfelter, Sherwood G, and Mayers, Marvin K. *Ministering Cross-Culturally: An Incarnational Model for Personal Relationships*. Grand Rapids, MI: Baker Book House, 1991.

Linton, Ralph. *The Cultural Background of Personality*. New York: Appleton-Century-Crofts, Inc., 1945.

Mackin, Sandra. 'Multinational Teams: Smooth As Silk Or Rough As Rawhide?' *Evangelical Missions Quarterly* 28(2) (April 1992): 134–140.

Madeira, E. 'Roots of Bad Feelings: What the Locals Say.' *Evangelical Missions Quarterly* 19(2) (April 1983): 104.

Marantika, Chris. 'An Indonesian Leader Speaks Out to the Church in the West.' *Evangelical Missions Quarterly* 26(1) (January 1990): 10.

Maxwell, John. 'The Asian Way of Doing Business – Is It Really Any Different?' *Silver Kris* (January 1994): 30.

Naisbitt, John. *Global Paradox*. New York: Avon Books, 1995.

Naisbitt, John. *Megatrends Asia*. New York: Simon & Shuster Inc., 1996.

Nanus, Burt. *Visionary Leadership*. San Francisco: Jossey-Bass Publishers, 1992.

Negandhi, A. R. 'Comparative Management and Organization Theory: A Marriage Needed.' *Academy of Management Journal* 18(2): 334–343.

Nelson, M. L., ed. *Readings in Third World Missions: A Collection of Essential Documents*. Pasadena, CA: William Carey Library, 1978.

Nevius, John. *Planting and Development of Missionary Churches*. revised edition. Phillipsburg, PA: Presbyterian and Reformed Publishing House, 1958.

Nida, Eugene. *Customs and Culture*. Pasadena, CA: William Carey Library, 1979.

Ohmae, Kenichi. *Beyond National Borders: Reflections On Japan and the World*. Homewood, IL: Dow Jones-Irwin, 1987.

Ohmae, K. *The Borderless World*. New York: Harper Business, 1990.

Ohmae, K. *Triad Power: The Coming Shape of Global Competition*. New York: The Free Press, 1985.

Ott, C. 'Let the Buyer Beware.' *Evangelical Missions Quarterly* 29(3) (July 1993): 288.

Padilla, Rene and Hendricks, B. 'Mission in the 1990s: Two Views.' *International Bulletin of Missionary Research* 13(4) (1989): 146–152.

Pate, Larry. *From Every People*. Monrovia, CA: MARC, 1989.

Pettigrew, A. M. 'On Studying Organizational Cultures.' *Administrative Science Quarterly* 22(4) (December 1979): 370–581.

Plueddemann, James E. 'Culture, Learning and Missionary Training.' In *Internationalising Missionary Training*, pp. 217–230. Edited by William D. Taylor. Grand Rapids, MI: Baker Book House, 1991.

Ramachandra, V. 'The Honor of Listening: Indispensable for Mission.' *Evangelical Missions Quarterly* 30(4): 405.

Richard, H. L. 'Is Extraction Evangelism Still the Way To Go?' *Mission Frontiers Bulletin* (September-October 1996): 14–16.

Rowe, A. J. and Mason, R. O. *Managing With Style: A Guide To Understanding, Assessing, and Improving Decision Making*. San Francisco: Jossey-Bass, 1989.

Samuel, Vinay, and Corwin, C. 'Assistance Programs Require Partnership.' *Evangelical Missions Quarterly* 15(2) (April 1979): 99.

Schein, Edgar. *Organizational Culture and Leadership*. San Francisco: Jossey-Bass, 1992.

Schipper, G. 'Non-Western Missionaries: Our Newest Challenge.' *Evangelical Missions Quarterly* 24(3) (July 1988): 200.

Schwartz, G. J. 'It's Time To Get Serious About the Cycle of Dependence in Africa.' *Evangelical Missions Quarterly* 28(2) (April 1993): 126–130.

Segall, P. M. *Cross-Cultural Psychology: Human Behavior in Global Perspective*. Monterey, CA: Brooks/Cole, 1979.

Senge, Peter. *The Fifth Discipline: The Art and Practice of the Learning Organization*. New York: Doubleday, 1990.

Singer, M. *Intercultural Communication: A Perceptual Approach*. Englewood Cliffs, NJ: Prentice-Hall, 1987.

Sookhdeo, Patrick. *New Frontiers In Mission*. Australia: Paternoster Press, 1994.